J.M. Hagaman

The Blade Annual and History of Cloud County,

from its earliest settlement to the present day

J.M. Hagaman

The Blade Annual and History of Cloud County,
from its earliest settlement to the present day

ISBN/EAN: 9783337345068

Printed in Europe, USA, Canada, Australia, Japan

Cover: Foto ©ninafisch / pixelio.de

More available books at **www.hansebooks.com**

THE

BLADE ANNUAL

AND

HISTORY OF CLOUD COUNTY,

FROM

ITS EARLIEST SETTLEMENT TO THE PRESENT DAY.

WITH A SEPARATE HISTORY OF THE

Towns and Cities of the County.

---

tistics and Population, Climate and Resources;

. RAINFALL FOR 20 YEARS.

By J. M. HAGAMAN.
The First Settler

CONCORDIA, KANSAS:
BLADE STEAM PRINTING HOUSE.
1884

SHAFER, P B, House, Sign and ornamental painter, 2 doors south M E church

Woods & Co, General merchandise, south side 6th st west of Broadway.

Haskett & Son, General merchandise, south side 6th st west of Broadway.

Dunning, D T, Groceries, Provisions, Vegetables, Crockery &c &c, south side 6th st under BLADE office.

Robinson & McCrary, Hardware, Tin, stoves, &c, S W cor. Bro'dw'y and 6th st.

BURRUS J E, Realestate Agent, Loan broker, Burrus' block, S E corner 6th st and Broadway.

Savard, A, Jewelery, Clocks & watches, Burrus' block, 6th st.

Bell, Jas, Merchant Tailor, Burrus' block, 6th st.

Martin, Ed, Restaurant, Burrus' block on Broadway.

Herwick, J S, Groceries, vegetables, candies, &c., north side sixth street, between Washington and State streets.

ARCHER & MADDOX, Livery, Feed and Sale Stable, south of Burrus' b'k on B'dy.

Eaves, Jas A, Second hand furniture, stoves, &c, opposite Opera House, 6, st.

Eaves, J A, Barber shop, opposite Opera House.

PARR, J M, House, Sign, Ornamental painting, Frescoing, &c &c, 6th street east of Broadway.

Oulnusa & Taylor, Carpenters and Builders, south side 6th st east of Br'd'y

Deveny, H C, Tailor; south side 6th st west of Washington.

Perkins C W, Grocer, south side 6th st between Wash. and State streets.

Perry, Eben, Pianos and Organs, south side 6th st between Wash. and State sts.

CHAFFEE A B Justice of the Peace and Police Judge, office on 6th street.

Murry & Barnes, Druggists Old Land Office building north side of 6th street.

PRICE, M V. Veterinary Surgeon, office in Murry & Barnes' Drug store.

Glover Bros, Agricultural Implments, south-east corner 6th and Broadway.

Beauchamp, & Luttrell Druggist, south side 6th st east of BLADE office.

ROGERS J T & Co, Clothiers, south side 6th st east of BLADE office.

Tyner, J H, General merchandise, 1st door east of BLADE office.

Seyster, J, & Reeves, Clocks, Watches, Jewelry, &c. north side of 6th st. between Broadway and Washington.

Martin, Benj., Restaurant, north side of 6th street.

Lambert, Geor. Barber shop, north side 6th street betw'n Bro'd'y & Wash.

Lake, Benjamin, Harness, Saddlery, Turf goods, &c. north side 6th st. between Broadway and Washington ave.

CRANS, L J, *Attorney at Law,* practices in the State and Federal Courts and before the U. S. Land Office. Will be found at his home just southwest of the school building.

Johnson, Mrs. Boarding-house; east of Broadway south side of 6th st.

Cline, M. C. Groceries, vegetables, &c. east of Brodway and south side 6th st.

Harrison, Sisters, Millinery, south side 6th street between Broadway and Washington.

Avenue House, J Torr proprietor. S E corner 6th st and Lincoln Avenue.

Mangan, J M, Doctor. One door east of Avenue House, 6th street.

Brosseau, L P, Carpenter and Builder, shop 3 doors east of Avenue House 6th st.

Longworth & Vernon, Wind-engines, Pumps, piping &c; under Opera room.

BETOURNAY, C A, Grocer and Baker; N W corner Broadway and 6th street.

COKON, F L Hardware, Stoves, Tinware, North side 6th street, west of Broadway.

Martin, Bros. Groceries, flour, fruits, &c, north side 6th st between Broadway and Washington avenue.

Paradis & Cartney, Meat market, north side 6th st. between Bro'd'y and Wash.

CRANS, CHARLIE, dealer in choice and fancy Poultry; henery on residence lot of L J CRANS, south-west of school-building.

POSTON, B F buys and ships hogs.

TATE, JOHN, buys and ships hogs.

NUTTER, NATUS, buys and ships hogs.

KING, E W buys and ships hogs.

Lane, Mrs H S Fashionable dressmaker; one door south of Linney & Dobler.

Warren, C T, dealer in paints, brushes, south-west corner 5th and State street.

HALFERTY, A F Art Needle-work; at the residence of W N Dunning.

Judy, D H Insurance Agent.

MARTEL, AMBROSE All kinds of nursery Stock; office up stairs, next door east of BLADE office.

PETERSON & REID; Land and Insurance agents; over 1st Nat'l Bank.

Houston & Son, Land agents; opposite the BLADE office.

CARPENTER & PEPPERELL; real estate and Loan agents; office up stairs west of BLADE building.

HILLIS, H Realestate and Loan agent; office opposite BLADE building.

Cleary, John Plasterer, Calciminer.

Perry, Ed Plasterer, Calciminer.

Kennett, Homer, Loan Agent, up stairs in Sturges' building, south side 6th st.

Krumm, Wm, Carpenter and Builder, shop on Sixth, east of Broadway.

Marcotte, N, Brick Maker, yard bet'w C. B. and K. P. railroads.

Residents of Lincoln Township, Including City of Concordia.

MALES.

Allen, Wm
Allen, Scott
Allen, Frank
Aldrich, Mill
Albey, L J
Auston, Preston
Auston, John
Auston, Preston
Anderson, B R
Archer, C
Archer, C E
Atteburry, R
Atwood, F J
Abell, A F
Allendorfer, Chas
Betournay, P K
Betournay, P Jr
Betournay, C A
Burnside,
Burnside, Isiah
Burnside, Wm
Brownell, S
Barnes, J C
Bush, Geo
Brown, N B
Brown, H D
Brown, D L
Brown, George
Ball, Peter
Ball, Sol
Ball, W
Ball, James
Ball, C M
Ball, Geo
Bradford, A A
Barker, J
Beatty, Wm
Berard, A
Burns, W McK
Brewer, J P
Brewer, S D
Bricker, Laf
Burch, Wal
Belisle, E A
Bayless, L
Burrus, J E
Burrus, Hillis
Besse, H
Beebe, Jas
Barons, S E
Barons, J
Bogue, John
Babb, John
Babb, Wm
Babb, W A
Barker, John
Bryant, Wm
Bailey, Jas
Brosseau, L P
Bollnger, A B
Barcelo, Joe
Barcelo, A
Blowfield, A M
Bean, Pius
Brummette, Laf
Beauchamp, G A
Banks, A L
Bennett, Orrin
Burger, O

Bushnell, B
Beach, J S
Bushell, J S
Boster, Chas
Baskin, W W
Bowman, W W
Birdsall, D
Barrett, M
Becktel, Jos
Buyless, A
Buyless, C
Bracken, B F
Bracken, F F
Budreau, E S
Budreau, Lewis
Bommereau, Jas
Burns, H D
Brodalph, J W
Banker, John
Bland, Frank
Bruner, E A
Barbran, P
Blakley, Chas
Bargler, L M
Clark, O J
Clark, S D
Clark N F
Chapman, Jos
Conkling, J C
Chausel, A
Copeland, Lor
Clarkson, Thomas
Collett, Eli
Carlisle, Sam
Crans, L J
Crans, M
Crans, Chas
Chandler, Jul
Cox, R E
Cleary, J H
Chaffee, A B
Craig, W O
Craig, J R
Chase, John
Closen, Wm
Chamberlain, C T
Carpenter, C P
Carpenter, Wm
Carpenter, N E
Colley, ——
Chambers, G
Cartney, W G
Cottrell, Wm
Callor, J C
Cupp, Adam
Cady, John,
Church, Sam
Christie, Louis
Crafts, J M B
Christopherson, N E
Charpiat, Jos
Conner, Wm
Conner, Paul
Conner, Frank
Coleman, Ed
Collens, Fred
Chase, Glen
Crill, N
Chambers L
Carrol, Jas

Crider, John
Clay, P
Cobb, F E
Darling, Taylor
Dutton, Lewis
Dewade, Jno
Dawson, J R
Dick, L M
Dumas, Peter
Douglas, J R
Dumas, Fred
Dodson, J
Dicker, N
Dickey, P A
Duff, J C
Demers, Sam
Dabney, F K
Dungerson, A
Dunning, D T
Dunning, W N
Dawson, C
Dangerfield, W
Dey, J E
Doane, E L
Decoro, Jas
Davis, Al
Daub, H
Delane, Jas
Dennis, Wm
Durand, Paul
Eckhart, John
Embuy, T A
Eaves, Jas.
Ewing, Jno
Emery Wm
Elliott, J C
Elliott, John
Easterday, Wm
English, C J
Fox, Chas
Flitch, John
Fallardeau, L
Farmer, W
Farmer, H J
Frontinghouse, E
Frontinghouse, Levi
Fortmor, John
Froncour, Jas
Fisher, Carl
Fullerton, H
Forkes, J
Finley, H
Finley, S
Farmer, L
Fisher, Burt
Fortin, Thos
Fortin, Geo
Freeman, C
Frisbie, J J
Floyd, Chas
Frazel, Lewis.
Griffin, S N
Griffin, J R
Griffin, Lee
Gand, Jas
Grimes, I
Garver, H
Gessinger, N
Gurtney, A
Gafford, J A

OFFICIAL DIRECTORY--STATING SALARY

OFFICERS OF THE UNITED STATES.

President	CHESTER A. ARTHUR, New York	$50,000
Vice President (acting)	GEORGE F. EDMUNDS, New Hampshire,	8,000
Cabinet.. { Secretary State	F. T. FRELINGHUYSEN, New Jersey	8,000
Secretary Treasury	HUGH McCULLOH, Indiana	8,000
Secretary Interior	HENRY M. TELLER, Colorado	8,000
Secretary War	ROBT. T. LINCOLN, Illinois	8,000
Secretary Navy	W E CHANDLER, New Hampshire	8,000
Attorney General	B. H. BREWSTER, Pennsylvania	8,000
Postmaster General	FRANK HATTON, Iowa	8,000
Commissioner of Agriculture	GEO. B. LORING, Massachusetts	3,000
Speaker House	JOHN G. CARLISLE, Kentucky	8,000

Kansas Senators	{ J. J. INGALLS, of Atchison	5,000
	{ PRESTON B. PLUMB, of Emporia	5,000
Member of Congress, Fifth District	JOHN A. ANDERSON, of Manhattan	5,000

STATE OFFICERS.

Governor	GEO. W. GLICK, of Atchison.	$3,000
Lieutenant Governor	D. W. FINNEY, of Woodson	6
Secretary State	JAMES SMITH, of Marshall	2,000
Auditor	E. P. McCABE, of Graham	2,000
Treasurer	SAMUEL T. HOWE, of Marion	2,500
Supt. Public Instruction	H. C. SPEER, of Davis	2,000
Attorney General	W. A. JOHNSTON, of Ottawa	1,500

Chief Justice	ALBERT H. HORTON, of Atchison	$3,000
Associate Justices	{ DAVID J. BREWER, of Leavenworth	3,000
	{ D. M. VALENTINE, of Topeka	3,000

STATE OFFICERS ELECTED NOVEMBER, 1884.

Governor	JOHN A. MARTIN, of Atchison
Lieutenant Governor	A. P. RIDDLE, of Crawford.
Secretary State	E. B. ALLEN, of Sedgwick.
Auditor	E. P. McCABE, of Graham.
Treasurer	SAMUEL T. HOWE, of Marion.
Attorney General	S. B. BRADFORD, of Osage.
Supt. Public Instruction	J. H. LAWHEAD, of Bourbon.
Chief Justice	A. H. HORTON, of Atchison.
Associate Justice	W. A. JOHNSTON, of Ottawa

Judge District Court, 12th District	EDWIN HUTCHINSON, of Marshall	$2,500
State Senator, 29th District	I. D. YOUNG, of Mitchell	3
Representatives { 81st Dist.	G. M. KREGER, of Oakland township.	3
{ 82d Dist.	D. B. MOORE, of Summit township	3

Roster of City Officers, and Concordia Business Directory.

Mayor,	W. F. GROESBECK
Councilmen	Wm. CONNER
	FRED LA ROCQUE
	THOS. McGUIRE
	A. H. BOLINGER
	W. G. REID
City Attorney	THEODORE LAING
Marshal	GEO. W. RIGBY
Night Watch,	ED. LAW
Clerk	L. N. HOUSTON
Treasurer	F. J. ATWOOD

Business Directory.

Taylor & Neitzel, Druggists, first door west of BLADE office.

FRISBIE & POSTON, Butchers, south side 6th street between Broadway & Was

MARSHALL, C H, Boots and Shoes, Iron Clad, south side 6th street.

Wade, S, Blacksmith, south side 6th st. east of Broadway.

HANSON, H N, General Merchandise south side 6th street b'w t Br'd and W.

FIRST NATIONAL BANK, south east corner Washington and 6th street.

Concordia House, 1 door south of First National Bank.

Freeman, C C, Clocks, Watches, &c. 1 door east of First National Bank.

Redwine, W J, Gunsmith, Washington avenue, 2 doors south Corner drug store.

SHEARER, J S, Sewing Machines, 1 door south of Corner drug store.

Hull, P W & Son, Blacksmiths and Wagon Makers, Washington st., between 6th and 7th.

CONCORDIA NATIONAL BANK, N W corner Sixth and Washington streets.

Doane, E, Furniture store, 1 door north of Concordia National Bank.

Maddox & Son, General Merchandise, 2 doors north Concordia National Bank.

McECKRON, B H, Palace Drug Store, 3 doors north Concordia National Bank.

McKINNON & Co, Hardware. 4 doors north Concordia National Bank.

CHICAGO LUMBER Co., yard N W cor. Fifth and Washington streets.

Blair, Wm, Grain dealer, north of C. B. R. R. b't'n Washington & State sts.

Spalding, H M & Co, Merchant Mills, on the River.

Exchange Hotel, C Guilbert, prop., on S E cor. 5th and Washington streets.

American Hotel, C H Parsons, prop., Washington street between 5th and 6th.

Lamay, Thos, Harness, Saddles, &c., 1 door south of Exchange Hotel.

HAGAMAN, W H, Brunswick Restaurant and confectioneries, Wash. Ave.

Simmons & Wilson, Furniture, Carpets, east side Washington Avenue.

CRIDER, John, Groceries, east side of Wash. ave., between 5th and 6th sts.

Banks, L M, Barber shop, east side of Washington ave., between 5th and 6th.

BARCELO, A, Livery, Feed and Sale Stable, south side Fifth street, between Washington and Broadway.

GREENE, J, Lumber, yard S W corner 5th and Broadway.

Short, W T, Carpenter & Builder, N side 5th b't'n Washington and Broadway

Whitehead, Abe, Livery, Feed & Sale Stable, north side 5th street.

Nelson A Blacksmith, N E corner 5th and Broadway.

Tate, Thomas, Livery, Feed and Sale Stable, 5th st., east of Broadway.

Mulit, H S, Photographer, south side 6th between Washington and State.

Beach, J S & Co, Hardware, Stoves, Tinware, Groceries, &c., south side 6th between Washington and State.

Watson & Twitchell, General Implements, pumps, wind mills, piping, &c., 1 door west of Concordia National Bank, south side 6th street.

McGuire, Tho Carpenter and Builder, first door south of Methodist church.

Moore, Edwin, Groceries, north side 6th st betw'n Wash and State streets.

Miller, Carl J Marble works, N. side 6th st 3 doors east of State street.

OPENHEIMER, M Groceries, Vegetables Flour, &c n s 6th st 2 doors east of State

Harkness, J S General merchandise, north-6th st 2 doors east of Wash. st.

GROESBECK, W F & Co General Groceries, Crockery, &c north-east corner 6th and Washington streets.

Howell, Bros. Lumber dealers, yard N E corner Fifth and State Streets.

Mohr, Geor & Co, Boots and Shoes, 1 door west of post office.

Shearer, J S, Books, and Stationery, Post office building.

GAY, A, Druggist, south-east corner 6th and Washington streets.

B & M Hotel, east side of Broadway, on B & M Railroad.

Gay, A	Jarvis, J	Lord, Chas
Gouche, O D	Jenkins, E J	Lamb, John
Guilbert, C	Jenkins, M J	Lewis, C
Grilly, J M	Johnson, Geo	Linblom, C
Grilly, N B	Johnson, Albert	Lucas, Geo
Geiger, J H	Johnson, Martin	LaRocque, Fred
Gifford, Fred	Johnson, Alaf	Law, E M
Goodrich, C C	Johnson, J H	Linney, E
Goodrich, John	Johnson, Frank	Light, H S
Goodrich, N	Johnson, John	Lathrop, A
Goodwin, Laf	Judy, D H	Lock, E R
Goodwin, John	Jackson, Theo	Low, Alfred
Gould, G A	Jackson, Albert	Monard, Jas
Groesbeck, W F	Jones, M V	Meris, E
Galer, C S	Jupe, Wm	McMillan, H
Godfrey, T J	Jordon, Wm	Misell, R
Glenn, P P	Joseph, E M	Mitchell, C
Hodges, J N	Kennett, Homer	McKinnon, M
Hall, Jos	Kennett, Wm	Martin, Harry
Hall, L D	Kelly, D J	Martin, Albert
Hull, P W	Kelly, Wm	Martin, Hector
Hull, Chas	Kelly, Harrison	Martin, Ed
Hunter, C C	Kelley, Marion	Martin, Geo
Hunter, Wm	Kenley, H E	Martin, E A
Hanson, H N	Kenley, J M	Martin, Fred
Hanson, Henry	Kerwick Louis	Martin, Eli
Haward, F E	Kelsey, H	Martin, August
Haward, R E	Kyle, Isaac	Martin, Ben
Haskett, W H	Kyle, Geo	Martin, Madore
Haskett E C	Kyle, Levi	Martin, Edmund
Hartmaire, R	Klinefelter, J M	Miller, Mart
Harrison, J M	Kenworthy, ——	Miller, John
Harrison, J B	Kunkle, F	Miller, Carl
Harris, J S	Kerwick, A M	Miller, Geo
Hibbon, Levi	Kelly, M J	Miller, Si
Harkness, J S	Kimball, Geo	Miller, Elza
Houston, S D Sen	Kimball, Otis	Miller, Harrison
Houston, S D Jr	Kruum, Wm	Miller, Lewis
Houston, L N	Kinmann, C P	McGuire, Thos
Holden, J P	King, E W	Monahan, J A
Howard, Jas	Kephart, C	Marcotte, F L
Haskin, W A	Kinney, S H	Marcotte, N
Hubbard, J B	Karnell, P A	Morgan, W S
Hedglan, ——	Kulp, Jacob	Monroe, L C
Hunter, C H	Lanoue, H	Messeldine, D
Hayden, C M	Lanoue, M	Millapex, Jas
Hayden, W T	Lanoue, P	Morgan, D
Hardin, J J	Lambert, G	McIntosh, J W
Hinkle, W C	Ladd, A D	McIntosh, J O
Hollis, Sol	Lavique, Geo	Marshall, Geo
Hinman, C	Lemons, S M	Marshall, C B
Hostetler, C F	Lemons, C M	Marshall, Chas
Hillis, H	Leonard, ——	McDonalds, ——
Herwick, J S	Leslie, J H	McCrary, S R
Healy, T A	Leundrie, F	McCrary, R S
Hill, Jas	Lamay, Thos	Morris, Ed
Hagaman, J M	Laing, Theo	Morris, Al
Hagaman, W H	Lemoine, Hurld	McLain, A
Herne, L H	Lemoine, H	Myers, John
Hale, E P	Lake, Benj	Missell, Ed
Hughes, T C	Linton, John	Mohr, Geo
Howard, B M	Linton, S	Martell, P
Hamilton, Rob	Lacksman, ——	Martell, Ambrose
Hawkins, W H	Luttrell, G M	Mulit H S
Hawkins, C R	Laque, H	Moore, J
Hicks ——	Longworth, E L	McEckron, B H
Honey, H R	Lamberson, C O	Molthrop, M
Hitt, Milton	Laque, H	Mosburg, J
Irvin, Levi	Lesage, Jos	Mosburg, Wm
Irving, Gid	LaFleche, Z R	Mosburg, John
Jennings, E	Lawrence, Thos	Maddox, M
Jarvis, H	Lord, P N	Michael, Chas

Maddox, Wm	Roswell J P	Sheafor, J W
McVey, Frank	Rose, Geo	Shafer, P B
McCoy, H C	Ray, Henry	Shafer, E B
McCoy, J T	Richards, C	Sanders, G L
Mercer, G J	Robinson, C	Seuse, C
Moore, E W	Rice, Lyman	Souter, Wm
Murray, Chas	Robinson, John	Signor, Wm
Morrison, John	Robinson, John	Southern Tod
Messick, H L	Rigby, Jos	Snyder, John
McCoursey, Wm	Rigby, Geo	Sagerty, Geo.
McDonald, C W	Rigby, J A	Silvey, Jeff
Morgan, Chas	Rankin, J M	Silvey, C
Miran, R	Ramage, D	Sargent, L H
Messer, A	Redwine, W J	Sargent, Frank
Nelson, A	Reid, W C	Shoemaker, H C
Nelson, P L	Reid, John	Sweet, C E
Neitzel, F W	Reid, Robt	Seyster, J
Neitzel, W F	Reid, W E	Seyster, I
Neitzel, Herman	Rines, C S	Shaver, Wm
Neitzel, August	Rogers, J	Strawbridge, M
Nye, Chas	Rogers, M	Simmons, D W
Newell, Frank	Revecan, Jos	Scott, Fred
Nadeau, C	Randall, J C	Spencer, Milton
Nadeau, A	Randall, E D	Sawhill, T A
Neal, M	Ralf, Lewis	Sawhill, W F
Neely, J N	Rains, T E	Sturges, F W
Nutter, Natus	Ramsey, O	Shabb, Frank
Newkirk, J	Reynolds, E	Sprague, S R
O'Neil, Jas	Reed Geo	Searl, Geo
Ouray, Wm	Root, W T	Stackhouse, D M
O'Haara, T	Ritchey, H	Stackhouse, John
Owen, Thos	Reeves, M E	Shumm, Geo
Oppenheimer, M	Ramsey, E S	Stewart, C W
Orput, J C	Revord, John	Tester, Alex
Peterson,	Shivers, W H	Tinian, Louis
Peterson, John	Swearngin, E E	Trombly, D
Peterson, J W	Swearngin, John	Trombly, R
Peterson, Geo	Stetson, C A	Trombly, E
Price, M V	Stetson, F C	Timmons, R M
Price, J J B	Shearer, H F	Timmons, ——
Perkins, C C	Shearer, J S	Timmons, Geo
Pfleiderer, J K	Short, W T	Taylor, S W
Phillips, David	Short, Rheuben	Talyor, W H
Pellitus, Geo	Sheltorley, Wm	Taylor, G M
Pellitus, ——	Smith, D J	Talyor, John
Pierson, W F	Smith, Clark,	Taylor, Wm
Paillet, Frank	Smith, Jas	Torr, Jasper
Paradis, J C	Smith, Fred	Thorp, J S
Pratt, S H	Smith, Stokes	Twitchell, C
Palmer, Geo	Smith, Geo	Townsdin, W S
Pottenger, N E	Smith, Walter	Titterington, H
Poston, B F	Smith, L M	Trombly, Fred
Pepperell, W. H L	Smith, David	Throop, Wm
Ponto, Lewis,	Smith, S H	Tabbot, Rob
Poal, Oliver,	Smith, J J	Throop, Louis
Perrier, Jos	Spurlock, S M	Throop, Jas
Perry, E A	Sieburt, H	Thomas, D W
Perry, Eben	Scorrum, F J	Thomas, N W
Parch, L D	Starkey, Caleb	Tate, Thos
Pennock, C	Starkey, Geo	Tate, John
Pennock, Al	Starkey, Jas	Tippin, L D
Parker, Peter	Schroff, W C	Tettler, Geo
Ponchire, Chas	Schroff, J F	Trude, H C
Plear, John	Spaulding, A H	Vielass A L
Polhemus, M	Spalding, H M	Veatch, J M
Prince, E	Seavey, John	Vinney, R B
Parr, J M	Stearns, C	Varbel, Caster
Rodes, Dan	Stearns, C H	Vernon, E T
Ross, G A	Stearns, Al	Whitehead, A
Ross, ——	Sterling, J C	Weaver, Clement,
Ross, Nathaniel	Samson, J M	Weaver, G L
Richey, J P	Sheafor, M V B	White, Geo

Weatherhead, I.
Williams, W S
Williams, B S
Williams, W H
Wyraff, R
Welch, Patrick
Webb, D C
Wait, David
Wait, Frank
Wait, Beard
Wade, Seneca
Wells, W H
Waldron, H
Ward, Julius
Wood, W
Woods, J P
Widner, John
Wilson, John
Wilson, D C
Walder, R
Watson, J
Warner, C S
Whipp, C W
Whipp, Wm
Young, Ed
Young, N S
Young, Jas
York, Geo

LINCOLN TOWNSHIP
[outside of city.]

Alexander, D J
Alexander, C H
Blair, Wm
Bevan, Henry
Bethel, John
Bennett, A H
Brannam, C
Bassett, Cla
Burns, J J
Burns, Hiram
Burns, Thos
Bryan, E A
Bryan, Wm
Bertraud, John
Belgard, A
Bender, B F
Babcock, C W
Bartlet, Elmer
Bassett, A L
Bushey, Fred
Charoness, R
Caleman, D H
Chickbrow, H
Chickbrow, Wm
Cross, Arlando
Coughlen, R
Cole, Wm
Cummons, Clark
Clark, C O
Clark, Milton
Clark, Herschell
Delver, G J
Driscoll, John
Driscoll, Dennis
Davis, C L
Davis, Allen
Davis, Henry
Davis, A N
Dotson, James
Dryes, J H
Demarlean, Dlos

Darling, J R
Dykes, F
Ells, Lewis
Easter, Wm
Flitch, Geo
Finch, Silverton
Fulmer, M
Foster, T M
Fruits, Geo
Groosbeck, B F
Glasby, Chas
Goen, Nelson
Hibner,
Hanna, John
Hartman, Martin
Henry, David
Hindman, F J
Jones, G W
Jones, R
Jones, S P
Jones, J W
Jones, H
Jupe, Amiel
King, S G
Kiser, O
Lewis, J M
Lewis, F W
Lewis, S R
Lavalbrye, M
Laypale, Geo
Leonard, Orland
Levreau, Peter
Merica, Silvanus
Mackley, John
Mackley, E A
Mackley, J B
Moore, C F
Narcotte, N
Matthew, Flaviors
Mintz, L D
Martin, Law
Messeldine, D
Moore, J
Naltiux, N
Newkirk, J
Palmer, John
Patrick, W S
Pierce, Fred
Reed, Wm
Rohston, C W
Roestson, David
Rogers, Thos
Rogers, Noah
Rhodes, Dan
Rambo, John,
Robins, John
Roberts, John
Rambo, Geo
Rambo, Chas
Springstead, J
Springstead, Geo
Shrader, W S
Sparks, Wm
Stone, Robert
Sprague, Alva
Starr, D A
Suppenfield, J R
Sears, Johnathan
Smith, W B
Shouse, John
Shaw, Ralf
Townsdin, John.

Townsdin, Jas
Townsdin, Chas
Townsdin, Geo
Towdsdin, Sam
Temple, Job
Trude, H
Truesdell, Jesse
Tresham, Viu
Trombly, Jas
Tatro, Paul
Vansickle, C
Wyckoff, Com
Ward, Dan
Wilmart, W H
Wright, W H
Wheeler, Ed
Walker, Jos

RAINFALL IN CLOUD CO.
For 24 Years.

1860	13¾*	inch
1861	36†	"
1862	35	"
1863	34	"
1864	33	"
1865	32	"
1866	31	"
1867	35	"
1868	18	"
1869	30	"
1870	28	"
1871	32	"
1872	26	"
1873	30	"
1874	22	"
1875	27	"
1876	29	"
1877	20	"
1878	29¼	"
1879	30¼	"
1880	18	"
1881—Total snowfall 28 in., rain and melted snow	16¼	"
1882	19¼	"
1883	21½	"
1884	16¾	"

*At Manhattan. No record kept here.
† Fractions less than ¼ an inch are omitted. Over ¼ are counted an inch.

OFFICERS REPUBLICAN LAND DISTRICT SINCE ITS LOCATION, OCTOBER, 1870.

Amos Cutter, of Mass., Register.
E. J. Jenkins, of Doniphan county, Kansas, Receiver.
B. H. McEckron, of Cloud county, Kansas, Register.
S. H. Dodge, of Mitchell county, Kansas, Register.
Thomas Wrong, of Cloud county, Kansas, Receiver.

ATTORNEYS.

L. J. Crans,	A. A. Carnahan,
M. V. Jones,	F. W. Sturges,
N. E. Carpenter,	E. J. Jenkins,
N. B. Brown,	C. W. McDonald,
C. W. Stewart,	H. Hillis,
D. L. Brown,	J. W. Sheafor,
Theo. Laing,	Thos. Wrong,
B. R. Anderson,	S. D. Houston, Jr.,
	J. W. Peterson.

PHYSICIANS.

F. L. Marcotte,	T. E. Rains,
C. H. Hunter,	L. D. Hall,
E. I. Kirk,	W. F. Sawhill,
F. K. Dabney,	Mrs. S. L. K. Honey,
D. W. Else,	C. W. Whipp,
A. Gay,	J. M. Mangan.

VETERINARY SURGEONS.

M. V. Price,   Joseph Becktel.

DENTISTS.

C. M. Bremerman,   C. C. Hinman,

County, Township and school district indebtedness, June 30, 1884:

County	$94,000
Townships	91,000
46 school districts	50,019

STANDARD RAILWAY TIME.

INTERCOLONIAL--60th Meridian.

All places east of *Maine* and Quebec.

EASTERN --75th Meridian.

Canada, between Quebec and Detroit,— *U. S.*, east of Buffalo, *N. Y.;* Pittsburg, *Pa.;* Wheeling and Huntington, *W. Va.;* Bristol, *Tenn.;* Charlotte, *N. C.*, and Augusta, *Ga.*

CENTRAL--90th Meridian.

West from "Eastern" limits, as above, to Broadview, *Canada;* to the Missouri River in *Dakota;* North Platte and McCook, *Neb.;* Wallace and Dodge City, *Kansas;* Toyah and Sanderson, *Texas.*

MOUNTAIN - 105th Meridian.

West from "Central" limits to Heron, *Montana;* Ogden, *Utah;* Needles and Yuma, *Arizona.*

PACIFIC -- 120th Meridian.

West from " Mountain " limits to coast.

ALMANAC TIME IS LOCAL TIME.

SUN time is, necessarily, the standard for Almanac calculations, because it gives, by a few chosen parallels of latitude, proper figures for all places on such lines — the march of the sun westward bringing the same hour regularly to each place to meet the phenomena.

Any almanac calculations based on "railroad" time would have to be changed for every mile. east or west, and would create absurd confusion, even if practicable.

When the difference between the "standard" and local time is known, there is no trouble in adding to or taking so much from the ALMANAC time, to bring it to " standard."

Almanacs and almanac time are more than ever before necessary, on account of this change of time for ordinary purposes of daily life.

A WINTER'S DAY.—Miss Edwards.

ECLIPSES, Etc.

In the year 1885 there will be four Eclipses—two of the Sun and two of the Moon.

I. An Annular Eclipse of the Sun, on March 16, visible as a Partial Eclipse over the United States generally, and as an Annular Eclipse from latitude 36 degrees on the Pacific Coast, in a northeasterly direction, to Hudson Bay in latitude 71 degrees.

II. A Partial Eclipse of the Moon, March 30, invisible in the United States.

III. A Total Eclipse of the Sun, September 8, invisible in the United States; visible in the southern part of South America, and in a part of Australia.

IV. A Partial Eclipse of the Moon, September 23 and 24, visible generally in the United States.

PLANETS BRIGHTEST.

Mercury, on January 26, before sunrise; April 8, after sunset; May 25, before sunrise; August 16, after sunset; September 15, before sunrise; November 30, after sunset.

Venus, though very bright in the latter part of the year, does not reach her greatest brilliancy until after the end of the year. Mars, not brightest this year. Jupiter, on February 19. Saturn, on December 26.

MORNING AND EVENING STARS.

Morning Stars.—Mercury, from January 3 to March 13, and from April 27 to June 27, and from September 2 to October 16, and from December 11 to the end of the year. Venus, until April 27.

Evening Stars.—Mercury, from March 13 to April 27, and from June 27 to September 2, and from October 16 to December 11. Venus, from April 27 to the end of the year. Mars, Jupiter, and Saturn, from January 1 to June 30.

THE FOUR SEASONS.

Winter begins December 21, 1884, at 4.25 A. M., and lasts 89 days and 56 minutes.

Spring begins March 20, 1885, at 5.21 A. M., and lasts 92 days, 20 hours and 22 minutes.

Summer begins June 21, 1885, at 1.43 A. M., and lasts 93 days, 14 hours and 25 minutes.

Autumn begins September 22, 1885, at 4.8 P. M., and lasts 89 days, 18 hours and 11 minutes.

Winter begins December 21, 1885, at 10.19 A. M.

Tropical year, 365 days, 5 hours and 54 minutes.

MOVABLE FEASTS.

Septuagesima Sunday	February 1
Sexagesima Sunday	" 8
Quinquagesima Sunday	" 15
Ash Wednesday	" 18
Quadragesima Sunday	" 22
Mid-Lent	March 15
Palm Sunday	" 29
Good Friday	April 3
Easter Sunday	" 5
Low Sunday	", 12
Rogation Sunday	May 10
Ascension Day	" 14
Whit Sunday	" 24
Trinity Sunday	" 31
Corpus Christi	June 4
Advent Sunday	Nov. 29

CYCLES.

Dominical Letter	D
Epact	14
Golden Number	5
Solar Cycle	18
Roman Indiction	13
Julian Period	6598
Dionysian Period	214
Jewish Lunar	2

LATEST U. S. POSTAL REGULATIONS.

There are four classes of domestic mail matter, divided as follows:

FIRST CLASS.—*a*, letters; *b*, matter partly in print and partly in writing; *c*, packages so wrapped that their contents can not be readily examined. Two cents per half ounce.

SECOND CLASS.—Newspapers, magazines and other periodicals, issued at stated intervals not exceeding three months, and not designed primarily for advertising purposes. One cent for each four ounces.

THIRD CLASS.—Books, transient newspapers, periodicals, circulars, proof-sheets and manuscript accompanying same, and printed matter generally (except that belonging in the second class). Upon matter of this class, or on its wrapper, the sender may write his own name, preceded by the word "from"; may mark any printed passage to call attention to it; may write date, address and signature of circulars, correct typographical errors, and write on cover or blank leaf of any book or other printed article of this class a simple dedication or presentation inscription not in the nature of personal correspondence. One cent for each two ounces.

FOURTH CLASS.—Merchandise and other articles not liable to damage other mail matter. Upon this matter the sender may write his name and address, preceded by the word "from," and may also write the quantities and names of articles inclosed. One cent for each ounce.

UNMAILABLE.—Liquids, poisons, explosives, ointments, pastes, fresh fruits and vegetables, animals alive or dead; articles having an offensive odor, obscene and indecent books, prints or other like articles.

MISCELLANEOUS INFORMATION.—Letters and postal cards directed to a person who has removed, or is temporarily absent from his usual place of residence, will be forwarded, on his request, free of charge; but *drop* letters can not be forwarded to other post-offices except on further prepayment to an amount sufficient (with that already prepaid) to cover postage at three cents per half ounce. Postal-cards bearing on their face side any message, written or printed, other than the address, are unmailable, and will be returned to the senders.

FOREIGN MAILS, ETC.—Letters for foreign countries, composing the "Universal Postal Union," five cents for each half ounce—prepayment optional. Newspapers and other printed matter (including books, pamphlets, commercial papers, photographs, sheet-music, maps, engravings, deeds, legal papers, and all documents wholly or partly in writing, and not in the nature of personal correspondence), and on samples of merchandise, one cent for each two ounces.

CANADA (including Nova Scotia, New Brunswick, Manitoba and Prince Edward's Island—letters, two cents for each half ounce; transient printed matter, one cent for each two ounces; second-class matter, same as in the United States; samples of merchandise (no dutiable articles or articles of intrinsic value admitted), ten cents for each package, not exceeding eight ounces in weight—prepayment compulsory.

REGISTRATION.—Letters and packages can be registered on payment of ten cents and full postage. The name and address of the sender must be indorsed by him on each letter or package. Mail matter may be sent registered to any post-office in the United States, Canada, or in any of the countries of the "Universal Postal Union."

MONEY ORDERS.—Money orders, limited to $5 each, payable in the United States, can be obtained at any post-office.

POSTAL NOTES payable to bearer for any sum from 1 cent to $4.99, inclusive, may be obtained at any money-order office payable at any other money-order office in the United States which the sender may designate. The fee for a postal note is 3 cents.

MY FIRST FRIEND.—After F. Barzaghi.

THE BISHOP.—Bricher.

GRAND MENAN ISLAND lies off the coast of Maine, a little below Eastport, on the western side of the entrance to the Bay of Fundy, which it narrows very materially. Carrying to an extreme that rocky character of the coast in which some of the Eastern States so widely differ from the sandy-coasted and low-beached Middle and Southern States, the Grand Menan almost creates the idea of having been misplaced by Nature—cut off, say, from some portion of the wild and rock-bound scenery of the British Islands, around which the surf rages so differently from what it possibly can do against the shelving and unresistive sand of the lower latitudes, and of much of the Western continent even of the higher. "The Bishop" is a detached pillar of rock, whose gently inclined outline seems to greet the returning voyager. The Bay of Fundy is remarkable for its high tides, the tidal wave or bore, as it is called, often overtaking swine who are feeding on the shellfish, as

| 1st Mo. | JANUARY. | | 31 days. |

Year Da.	Month Da.	Week Da.	Moon Wanes M'ns	Sun Rises	Sun Sets	Moon Rises	Moon Passes
			H. M.	H. M.	H. M.	H. M.	
1	1	Th	12 4 6	7 19	4 49	rises.	
2	2	Fr	12 4 34	7 19	4 49	6 59	
3	3	Sa	12 5 2	7 19	4 50	8 0	
4	4	M	12 5 29	7 19	4 51	9 16	
5	5	M	12 5 55	7 19	4 52	10 20	
6	6	Tu	12 6 22	7 19	4 53	11 25	
7	7	W	12 6 47	7 19	4 54	morn	3 Q.
8	8	Th	12 7 13	7 19	4 55	0 22	
9	9	Fr	12 7 35	7 19	4 56	1 20	
10	10	Sa	12 8 2	7 19	4 57	2 16	
11	11	M	12 8 25	7 19	4 58	3 11	
12	12	M	12 8 48	7 18	4 59	4 4	
13	13	Tu	12 9 11	7 18	5 0	4 54	
14	14	W	12 9 32	7 18	5 1	5 42	
15	15	Th	12 9 54	7 17	5 2	6 26	
16	16	Fr	12 10 14	7 17	5 3	sets. N.	
17	17	Sa	12 10 34	7 17	5 4	6 39	
18	18	M	12 10 53	7 16	5 5	7 37	
19	19	M	12 11 11	7 16	5 6	8 36	
20	20	Tu	12 11 28	7 15	5 7	9 36	
21	21	W	12 11 15	7 15	5 8	10 37	
22	22	Th	12 12 1	7 14	5 9	11 39	
23	23	Fr	12 12 16	7 14	5 11	morn	1 Q.
24	24	Sa	12 12 30	7 13	5 12	0 42	
25	25	M	12 12 44	7 12	5 13	1 49	
26	26	M	12 12 56	7 12	5 14	2 55	
27	27	Tu	12 13 8	7 11	5 15	3 59	
28	28	W	12 13 19	7 10	5 16	5 0	
29	29	Th	12 13 29	7 9	5 17	5 55	
30	30	Fr	12 13 39	7 8	5 19	rises. F.	
31	31	Sa	12 13 47	7 8	5 20	6 52	

2d Mo. FEBRUARY. 28 days.

Year Day	Month Div	Week Day	Moon Rises or Sets.	Sun Rises	Sun Sets	Moon Rises	Moon Phase
					H. M.	H. M.	H. M.
32	1	M	12 13 55	7	5 21	8 0	
33	2	Tu	12 14 2	6 59	5 22	10 8	
34	3	W	12 14 8	6 58	5 23	11 8	
35	4	Th	12 14 14	6 57	5 24	morn	
36	5	Th	12 14 16	6 56	5 26	0 6	3 Q.
37	6	Fr	12 14 21	6 54	5 27	1 3	
38	7	Sa	12 14 23	6 53	5 28	1 3	
39	8	M	12 14 26	6 52	5 29	1 56	
40	9	M	12 14 25	6 50	5 30	2 18	
41	10	Tu	12 14 28	6 48	5 31	3 37	
42	11	W	12 14 29	6 47	5 32	4 22	
43	12	Th	12 14 27	6 45	5 34	5 5	
44	13	Fr	12 14 25	6 44	5 35	5 44	
45	14	Sa	12 14 23	6 42	5 36	sets.	N.
46	15	M	12 14 20	6 42	5 37	6 28	
47	16	M	12 14 16	6 41	5 38	7 29	
48	17	Tu	12 14 11	6 40	5 39	8 30	
49	18	W	12 14 6	6 48	5 40	9 33	
50	19	Th	12 14 0	6 42	5 41	10 36	
51	20	Fr	12 13 53	6 45	5 43	11 41	
52	21	Sa	12 13 46	6 44	5 44	morn.	
53	22	M	12 13 38	6 43	5 45	0 45	1 Q.
54	23	M	12 13 29	6 41	5 46	1 48	
55	24	Tu	12 13 20	6 40	5 47	2 48	
56	25	W	12 13 10	6 39	5 48	3 45	
57	26	Th	12 13 0	6 37	5 49	4 34	
58	27	Fr	12 12 49	6 36	5 50	5 20	
59	28	Sa	12 12 37	6 34	5 51	rises.	F.

it rushes with the speed of an express train from the ocean, rising from 40 to 60 ft. The bay is deep, but of difficult navigation; it is 170 miles long and from 30 to 50 miles wide.

THE SCIENCE OF THE EARTH has been the subject of philosophical speculation from the time of Homer, and this science is said to have been cultivated in China many ages before the Christian era. When the theories and discoveries of geologists were first propounded, they were condemned as being opposed to the statements of the Bible; but in this enlightened age the Christian astronomer and geologist, in proportion as their minds are expanded by scientific investigation, see the necessity of demonstrating that there is no collision between the discoveries in the natural world and the inspired record.

ALMANACS, or other books with calendars, have been popular for many centuries. Regiomontanus is supposed to have been indebted for his formulæ of 1474, to the Persian almanacs. John Somer's Calendar, written in Oxford, Eng., was published as early as 1380. The almanac was canonized as St. Almachius in the Roman calendar. The pop-

ular almanac in Shakspeare's time was published by Leonard Digges. In 1851 Dr. McGowan, laboring in China for the Missionary Union, prepared a philosophical almanac in the language of that country, exhibiting to the Chinese the realities of science, and particularly detailing the principles of the magnetic telegraph. Moore's Almanac, first published in England in 1713, reached an annual sale of upwards of 500,000 copies. In the British Museum and universities are some curious specimens of early almanacs.

THE smallest circular saw in practical use is a disk about the size of a five-cent piece, being employed for cutting slits in gold pens. They are about as thick as ordinary paper, and make 400 revolutions per minute, this high speed keeping them rigid, notwithstanding their extreme thinness.

THE GRAND TRIANON, the palace at Versailles where the unfortunate Marie Antoinette used to give the famous parties which her enemies described as orgies, is an elegant outpost of its kingly neighbor, to whose magnificent grounds its own, fully as beautiful, are joined. Bounded by a fine hedge, many beautiful vistas are opened in every direction, the gaps being protected by ditches which are not noticeable until one is almost upon them. The statuary and fountains, though on a smaller scale than those of the king's palace, are very beautiful, and no more fitting scene for the gallantries of those days could be imagined. Here, on October 5, 1789, the mob invaded the privacy of the queen, and only her own intrepidity saved her from violence.

THERE are 3,985 paper mills in the world, producing every year 959,000 tons of clean paper. About one-half is printed on, and the other half is used for writing paper. Annually the various Government departments consume about 100,000 tons in official business, the schools 90,000 tons, commerce 120,000 tons, industry 90,000 tons, and private correspondence in all only 90,000 tons.

THE FARMERS' .ETS.—Specht.

THIS PICTURE OF RABUN GAP furnishes but an inference of the many lovely views to be seen in Northern Georgia. The locality is very picturesque, composed of sloping hills, fertile valleys and winding streams, and is becoming a great resort for the pleasure-seeking public. All the way down the valley of the Tennessee River to Knoxville, and westward to Chattanooga and Huntsville, the scenery is most varied and charming, while the historic associations cluster thickly on every hand. Lookout Mountain is a grand point for tourists, not only as one of the great landmarks of history, but as well for the natural beauties and the exhibit of the changes being wrought by recent enterprise and awakened activity, such as may now be witnessed in so many parts of the Great South. The sides of this famous old mountain are seamed and scarred by the onset and clash of almighty forces, in contests which belittle the fiercest battles of man. Through the tangled forest and over the precipitous rocks dash waters of silvery purity, and a day's tramp will discover many unknown and neglected falls, which, if in the White Mountains or Catskills, would have been sung by poets and embalmed in our literature. Since the manifest improvement during the past decade in the Southern railroad system these regions are becoming better known.

3d Mo.   MARCH.   31 days.

Year Day	Month Day	Week Day	Moon Wash'ton M. Time	Sun Rises	Sun Sets	Moon Rises	Moon Phase
			H. M. S.	H. M.	H. M.	H. M.	
60	1	I	12 12 25	6 33	5 52	6 44	
61	2	M	12 12 13	6 32	5 53	7 49	
62	3	Tu	12 12 0	6 30	5 54	8 51	
63	4	W	12 11 16	6 29	5 55	9 52	
64	5	Th	12 11 32	6 27	5 56	10 50	
65	6	Fr	12 11 18	6 26	5 57	11 46	
66	7	Sa	12 11 3	6 24	5 58	morn.	
67	8	I	12 10 48	6 23	5 59	0 39	3 Q.
68	9	M	12 10 33	6 21	6 0	1 29	
69	10	Tu	12 10 17	6 20	6 1	2 16	
70	11	W	12 10 1	6 18	6 2	3 0	
71	12	Th	12 9 45	6 17	6 3	3 49	
72	13	Fr	12 9 28	6 15	6 4	4 18	
73	14	Sa	12 9 12	6 14	6 5	4 54	
74	15	I	12 8 54	6 12	6 6	5 28	
75	16	M	12 8 37	6 10	6 7	sets.	N.
76	17	Tu	12 8 20	6 9	6 8	7 23	
77	18	W	12 8 2	6 7	6 9	8 27	
78	19	Th	12 7 44	6 6	6 10	9 33	
79	20	Fr	12 7 26	6 4	6 11	10 38	
80	21	Sa	12 7 8	6 2	6 12	11 42	
81	22	I	12 6 50	6 1	6 13	morn	
82	23	M	12 6 32	5 59	6 14	0 42	1 Q.
83	24	Tu	12 6 13	5 58	6 15	1 38	
84	25	W	12 5 55	5 56	6 16	2 29	
85	26	Th	12 5 36	5 55	6 17	3 15	
86	27	Fr	12 5 18	5 53	6 18	3 56	
87	28	Sa	12 4 59	5 51	6 19	4 34	
88	29	I	12 4 41	5 50	6 20	5 10	
89	30	M	12 4 22	5 48	6 21	rises.	F.
90	31	Tu	12 4 4	5 47	6 22	7 36	

| 4th Mo. | | APRIL. | | | 30 days. | | |

Y. D.	Month D.	Week D.	Day's ...	Sun Rises	Sun Sets	Moon Rises	Moon Phase
			H. M.	H. M.	H. M.	H. M.	
91	1	W	12 3 46	5 45	6 23	8 36	
92	2	Th	12 3 28	5 44	6 24	9 34	
93	3	Fr	12 3 10	5 42	6 25	10 29	
94	4	Sa	12 2 52	5 40	6 26	11 21	
95	5	S	12 2 34	5 39	6 27	morn.	
96	6	M	12 2 17	5 37	6 28	0 9	
97	7	Tu	12 2 0	5 36	6 29	0 54	3 ◯
98	8	W	12 1 43	5 34	6 30	1 36	
99	9	Th	12 1 26	5 33	6 31	2 14	
100	10	Fr	12 1 10	5 31	6 32	2 50	
101	11	Sa	12 0 54	5 30	6 33	3 25	
102	12	S	12 0 38	5 28	6 34	3 59	
103	13	M	12 0 23	5 27	6 34	4 32	
104	14	Tu	12 0 8	5 25	6 35	5 8	
105	15	W	11 59 53	5 24	6 36	sets. N.	
106	16	Th	11 59 39	5 22	6 37	8 26	
107	17	Fr	11 59 25	5 21	6 38	9 32	
108	18	Sa	11 59 11	5 20	6 39	10 36	
109	19	S	11 58 58	5 18	6 40	11 35	
110	20	M	11 58 45	5 17	6 41	morn	
111	21	Tu	11 58 33	5 15	6 42	0 27	1 ◯
112	22	W	11 58 21	5 14	6 43	1 15	
113	23	Th	11 58 9	5 13	6 44	1 57	
114	24	Fr	11 57 58	5 11	6 45	2 35	
115	25	Sa	11 57 47	5 10	6 46	3 11	
116	26	S	11 57 37	5 9	6 47	3 45	
117	27	M	11 57 28	5 7	6 48	4 19	
118	28	Tu	11 57 18	5 6	6 49	4 53	
119	29	W	11 57 10	5 5	6 50	rises 6.	
120	30	Th	11 57 2	5 3	6 51	8 19	

THE UNAKAS, a range of mountains separating Tennessee from North Carolina, equaling the Rocky Mountains at many points in rugged grandeur, and, many say, excelling them in beauty. They are carpeted with grasses or covered with numerous varieties of ferns and mosses, or with the mountain laurel, spruce, balsam, and the rich, red rhododendron and azalia. The beautiful French Broad River, rising in North Carolina, and running North-west, after getting above the famous resorts of Asheville and Warm Springs, cuts through the base of the Unakas, which here attain a height of 5,000 feet on each side of the river. The railroad runs for more than fifty miles along this river, frequently crossing it on substantial bridges, and giving full and magnificent views of this unrivaled scenery.

ST. PETER'S AT ROME.—Perot.

PRE-EMINENT among the Christian temples of the world is St. Peter's, the work of many popes and architects, finally consecrated by Urban VIII. in 1626, which Gibbon calls "the most glorious structure that has ever been applied to the use of religion." Externally the work, though magnificent in materials and dimensions, is disfigured by the prominence of the front added by Maderno, which almost hides from the near spectator the principal feature—the vast and towering dome; while, had the original plan of Bramante and Michael Angelo been followed, the whole dome would have been visible from the square before the church. But the dome itself and the interior of the edifice are held to be unrivaled in magnitude, proportion and decoration. The building occupied 175 years. The length of the interior is 613½ feet; transept from wall to wall, 446½ feet; height of nave, 152½ feet. The dome, from the pavement to the base of the lantern, is 405 feet, to the top of the cross 448 feet.

The dome of the Capitol at Washington is 307½ feet to the top of the statue of liberty.

HORTICULTURISTS have demonstrated that the simplest flower that grows in the field can, through cultivation, be made to attain perfection. With most of us the love for floriculture is innate, and in accordance with the extent it is developed so is our refinement expressed. Owing to the invention of the green-house we are not deprived of flowers in Winter, but they seem most appropriate in the Spring time when all nature is alive to its duty. It is then that the gardens yield their most attractive beauties, affording lucrative occupation to women and girls, who display and sell their products on the streets in large quantities to passers by.

PREPARING FLOWERS FOR MARKET.— Robinson.

"THE BREAKING WAVES dashed high on the stern and rock-bound coast," but to the earnest, sea-toss'd Pilgrims how charming must have been the primitive glories of the mountains and rivers of New England! No wonder that her sons have ever thought of her with love and regret wherever their adventurous wanderings in search of fortune may have led. Other mountains may far o'ertop, other streams pour greater floods, but where are the charms of foliage and of clear purity that will rival these?

"Then, hurrah for old New England
And her cloud-capp'd granite hills!"

THE ancient Romans on May-day used to go in procession to the grotto of Egeria. May-day has also been immemorially observed in England as a rural festival; and May-poles are in many places profusely decorated with garlands wreathed in honor of the day. May received its name, some say, from Romulus, who gave it this appellation in respect to the Senators and nobles of his city, they being termed *Majores*. Others claim it was called from Maia, the mother of Mercury.

THE application of a strong solution of chromic acid three or four times a day by means of a camel's-hair pencil is the best and easiest method of removing warts.

Year Day	Month Day	Week Day	Moon. Wash ton M Time.			Sun Rises	Sun Sets	Moon Rises	Moon Phase
			H. M. S.			H. M.	H. M.	H. M.	
121	1	Fr	11 56 51			5 2	6 52	9 43	
122	2	Sa	11 56 47			5 1	6 53	10 3	
123	3	☽	11 56 41			5 0	6 54	10 50	
124	4	M	11 56 35			4 59	6 55	11 32	
125	5	Tu	11 56 29			4 58	6 56	morn	
126	6	W	11 56 25			4 57	6 57	0 12	
127	7	Th	11 56 21			4 56	6 57	0 48	3 ◯
128	8	Fr	11 56 17			4 54	6 58	1 23	
129	9	Sa	11 56 14			4 53	6 59	1 56	
130	10	☽	11 56 12			4 52	7 0	2 29	
131	11	M	11 56 10			4 51	7 1	3 3	
132	12	Tu	11 56 9			4 50	7 2	3 39	
133	13	W	11 56 8			4 49	7 3	4 18	
134	14	Th	11 56 8			4 49	7 4	sets.	N.
135	15	Fr	11 56 9			4 48	7 5	8 21	
136	16	Sa	11 56 10			4 47	7 6	9 25	
137	17	☽	11 56 11			4 46	7 7	10 22	
138	18	M	11 56 13			4 45	7 8	11 13	
139	19	Tu	11 56 16			4 44	7 8	11 57	
140	20	W	11 56 19			4 43	7 9	morn	
141	21	Th	11 56 23			4 43	7 10	0 37	1 ◑
142	22	Fr	11 56 27			4 42	7 11	1 14	
143	23	Sa	11 56 32			4 41	7 12	1 48	
144	24	☽	11 56 37			4 41	7 13	2 21	
145	25	M	11 56 43			4 40	7 13	2 54	
146	26	Tu	11 56 49			4 39	7 14	3 29	
147	27	W	11 56 56			4 39	7 15	4 5	
148	28	Th	11 57 3			4 38	7 16	rises.	F.
149	29	Fr	11 57 11			4 38	7 17	7 58	
150	30	Sa	11 57 19			4 37	7 17	8 46	
151	31	☽	11 57 28			4 37	7 18	9 30	

6th Mo.   JUNE.   30 days.

Year Day	Month Day	Week Day	Noon. Wash'ton M. Time. H. M. S.	Sun Rises H. M.	Sun Sets H. M.	Moon Rises H. M.	Moon Phase
152	1	M	11 57 36	4 36	7 19	10 11	
153	2	Tu	11 57 46	4 36	7 19	10 48	
154	3	W	11 57 55	4 36	7 20	11 23	
155	4	Th	11 58 6	4 35	7 21	11 56	
156	5	Fr	11 58 16	4 35	7 21	morn.	3 Q.
157	6	Sa	11 58 27	4 35	7 22	0 28	
158	7	S	11 58 38	4 35	7 23	1 1	
159	8	M	11 58 49	4 34	7 23	1 34	
160	9	Tu	11 59 1	4 34	7 24	2 11	
161	10	W	11 59 13	4 34	7 24	2 51	
162	11	Th	11 59 25	4 34	7 25	3 37	
163	12	Fr	11 59 37	4 34	7 25	sets.	N.
164	13	Sa	11 59 50	4 34	7 26	8 8	
165	14	S	12 0 3	4 34	7 26	9 4	
166	15	M	12 0 15	4 34	7 27	9 53	
167	16	Tu	12 0 28	4 34	7 27	10 36	
168	17	W	12 0 41	4 34	7 27	11 15	
169	18	Th	12 0 54	4 34	7 28	11 51	
170	19	Fr	12 1 7	4 34	7 28	morn.	1 Q.
171	20	Sa	12 1 20	4 34	7 28	0 24	
172	21	S	12 1 33	4 35	7 28	0 58	
173	22	M	12 1 46	4 35	7 29	1 31	
174	23	Tu	12 1 59	4 35	7 29	2 7	
175	24	W	12 2 12	4 35	7 29	2 45	
176	25	Th	12 2 24	4 36	7 29	3 25	
177	26	Fr	12 2 37	4 36	7 29	4 9	
178	27	Sa	12 2 49	4 36	7 29	rises.	F.
179	28	S	12 3 1	4 37	7 29	8 11	
180	29	M	12 3 13	4 37	7 29	8 49	
181	30	Tu	12 3 25	4 37	7 29	9 25	

MT. MANSFIELD. — Thos. Moran.

MOUNT MANSFIELD, as seen in our cut, is one of the noble peaks of the Vermont Green Mountains, and looms up grandly over the tertile plains and quiet loveliness of the Missisquoi. It is the highest mountain in Vermont, 4,279 feet above the sea. The mineral products of the Green Mountains are very valuable, including excellent iron ores, manganese, marble, slate, etc., proximity to a market giving value to products that would be lost for ages in the vast wilds of the Rockies and Sierras.

THE first prayer book of Edward VI. came into use by authority of Parliament on Whit-Sunday, 1549.

THE INDIGNANT ORPHANS. — Gustave Süs.

THIS terrier has evidently in a fit of rage orphaned an interesting brood, and then, as the leg and feathers imply, eaten his victim up. The poor motherless chicks are upbraiding him for his crime, and to judge from the expression of his face are producing in his mind a sense of remorse. In pictures of this kind Mr. Süs, of whose painting this is a reproduction, is well and favorably known to art lovers.

THE ENVIRONS OF FLORENCE, second in interest only to Rome and by many considered more attractive, are like beautiful gardens and abound in delightful places for excursions. There has for many years been quite a settlement of American genius hereabouts — sculptors and artists who for the healthful climate and art treasures, so nearly equal to those of the capital itself, prefer it for a place of residence. The Duomo, or cathedral church of Santa Maria del Fiore, is a vast and superb structure, which is surpassed in architectural grandeur only by St. Peter's at Rome. The length of the building is nearly 500 feet, and width of the united transepts 306 feet. The height of the nave is 153 feet. The dome of this cathedral is the largest in the world, its circumference being greater than that of St. Peter's, and its comparative height greater, though its base is not placed so high above the ground. From the pavement to the summit of the cross is 387 feet. This dome served as a model for that of St. Peter's.

MOONLIGHT NEAR FLORENCE, ITALY.

RIVER SCENERY OF THE BLUE RIDGE

FROM NORFOLK starts the first division of the great iron band which reaches from the Atlantic to the Pacific. Soon after leaving this enterprising seaport city, the tourist obtains evidence of Virginia's loveliness. Though time and change have plowed deep furrows in that beauty which gave the new-born earth its pristine grace, still Nature from her wondrous wealth impartially bestows unending favors on her worshippers; and o'er earth's wide expanse are favored spots never to be effaced. Through the southern portion of the State, passing along the sides of wooded crests, into emerald valleys and by rushing streams, the railway has developed a beautiful section.

7th Mo.			JULY.						31 days.
Year Day	Month Day	Week Day	Moon Was the H. min.		Sun Rises	Sun Sets	Moon Rises		Moon Phase
			H. S.	H. M.	H. M.	H. M.	H. M.		
182	1	W	12 3 36	4 38	7 29		9 58		
183	2	Th	12 3 48	4 39	7 29		10 30		
184	3	Fr	12 3 59	4 39	7 29		11 2		
185	4	Sa	12 4 9	4 40	7 29		11 34		
186	5	M	12 4 20	4 41	7 29		morn.	3 Q.	
187	6	M	12 4 30	4 41	7 29		0 8		
188	7	Tu	12 4 40	4 42	7 28		0 45		
189	8	W	12 4 49	4 42	7 28		1 27		
190	9	Th	12 4 58	4 43	7 27		2 15		
191	10	Fr	12 5 7	4 44	7 27		3 10		
192	11	Sa	12 5 15	4 44	7 26		4 12		
193	12	M	12 5 22	4 45	7 26		sets.	N.	
194	13	M	12 5 30	4 46	7 25		8 29		
195	14	Tu	12 5 36	4 46	7 25		9 11		
196	15	W	12 5 43	4 47	7 24		9 49		
197	16	Th	12 5 48	4 48	7 24		10 25		
198	17	Fr	12 5 53	4 49	7 23		10 59		
199	18	Sa	12 5 58	4 49	7 23		11 34	1 Q.	
200	19	M	12 6 2	4 50	7 22		morn		
201	20	M	12 6 6	4 51	7 21		0 9		
202	21	Tu	12 6 9	4 52	7 20		0 46		
203	22	W	12 6 11	4 53	7 20		1 25		
204	23	Th	12 6 13	4 54	7 19		2 8		
205	24	Fr	12 6 14	4 54	7 18		2 54		
206	25	Sa	12 6 14	4 55	7 17		3 43		
207	26	M	12 6 14	4 56	7 16		rises.	F.	
208	27	M	12 6 14	4 57	7 16		7 27		
209	28	Tu	12 6 12	4 58	7 15		8 1		
210	29	W	12 6 11	4 59	7 14		8 34		
211	30	Th	12 6 8	5 0	7 13		9 6		
212	31	Fr	12 6 5	5 0	7 12		9 37		

8th Mo.   AUGUST.   31 days.

Year Day	Month Day	Week Day	Noon. Wash'ton M. Time.	Sun Rises	Sun Sets	Moon Rises	Moon Phase
			H. M. S.	H. M.	H. M.	H. M.	
213	1	Sa	12 6 1	5 1	7 11	10 10	
214	2	M	12 5 57	5 2	7 10	10 44	
215	3	M	12 5 53	5 3	7 9	11 24	3 Q.
216	4	Tu	12 5 47	5 4	7 8	morn.	
217	5	W	12 5 41	5 5	7 7	0 7	
218	6	Th	12 5 35	5 6	7 5	0 57	
219	7	Fr	12 5 28	5 7	7 4	1 53	
220	8	Sa	12 5 20	5 8	7 3	2 56	
221	9	M	12 5 12	5 9	7 2	4 5	
222	10	M	12 5 3	5 9	7 1	sets.	N.
223	11	Tu	12 4 54	5 10	6 59	7 43	
224	12	W	12 4 44	5 11	6 58	8 21	
225	13	Th	12 4 33	5 12	6 57	8 57	
226	14	Fr	12 4 22	5 13	6 56	9 32	
227	15	Sa	12 4 11	5 14	6 54	10 8	
228	16	M	12 3 58	5 15	6 53	10 45	
229	17	M	12 3 46	5 16	6 52	11 24	1 Q.
230	18	Tu	12 3 33	5 17	6 50	morn.	
231	19	W	12 3 19	5 18	6 49	0 6	
232	20	Th	12 3 5	5 19	6 48	0 51	
233	21	Fr	12 2 50	5 19	6 46	1 39	
234	22	Sa	12 2 35	5 20	6 45	2 29	
235	23	M	12 2 19	5 21	6 43	3 23	
236	24	M	12 2 2	5 22	6 42	4 18	F.
237	25	Tu	12 1 47	5 23	6 40	rises.	
238	26	W	12 1 30	5 24	6 39	7 8	
239	27	Th	12 1 13	5 25	6 38	7 40	
240	28	Fr	12 0 55	5 26	6 36	8 13	
241	29	Sa	12 0 37	5 27	6 35	8 47	
242	30	M	12 0 19	5 28	6 33	9 24	
243	31	M	12 0 1	5 28	6 31	10 5	

New River is a stream noted for its beauty. Diverging from the main track of the Norfolk and Western Railroad at New River Station is a branch leading to the heart of the wonderful ore beds and coal fields about Pocahontas, in West Virginia. On this route are magnificent mountain views, which awaken the loftiest imaginations. By this line are opened new routes to Mountain Lake, Eggleston Springs, and the famous Red Sulphur Springs ; and while a first cause of construction was that easy access might be had to the marvelous wealth of the section traversed, yet it is certain that no less fame attaches to the romantic scenery here than to other Virginia resorts embalmed in song and story.

THE first daily newspaper printed in the United States was published in Boston on Sept. 25, 1791.

THE first use of a locomotive in this country was in 1829.

THE first steamboat plied the Hudson in 1807.

THE first horse railroad was built in 1826-27.

THE first balloon ascent was made in 1798.

KANNARRO CAÑON.

Kannarro is a small Mormon village in southern Utah, nestling at the foot of lofty mountains and near the terminus of the ranges extending south from Salt Lake City. The cañon is some six or eight miles south of the village, and it is in this cañon that the tourist receives the first hint of that glorious region to the south, the cañon of the Colorado River of the West. Here are first seen those wonderful masses of red sandstone that, a little further south, become overwhelmingly stupendous, staggering belief in their vastness and magnificent forms. Colburn's Butte is 2,000 feet high and of a brilliant vermilion hue. It is equally grand and beautiful in storm or sunshine.

In connection with this beautiful scenery we may call attention to the wonderful clearness of the Western atmosphere. Untainted by the smoke of great cities or fogs of the warm coast regions, it is clear and sparkling as a crystal, utterly deceptive as to distances; thirty or forty miles appear to a person, not accustomed to the region, as no more than eight or ten miles. The same optical delusion affects heights and depths, the novice being quite unable to approximate to correct measurements with the eye. The climate is lovely, though most of the country in these mountain valleys is a desert until irrigation is introduced. The numerous streams that flow from the mountains are finally lost in the parching soil, which is sandy and very absorbent.

ELEVEN thousand newspapers and periodicals are published in the United States. New York has the largest number of any State, viz., 1,411, and next comes Illinois with 1,017. Pennsylvania ranks third with 973, and afterwards, in order, are Ohio, Iowa and Missouri. Six hundred and forty of these papers are published in German, forty-nine in Danish and Scandinavian, and forty-one in French; five Welsh, three Chinese, three Indian and one in Irish.

SINCE the conquest of Mexico by Europeans there has been no cessation of work in the gold and silver mines of the country. Under Spanish rule, or from 1537 to 1821, the value of silver produced exceeded 10,431,348,515f., and that of gold 343,842,055f. Since the independence of Mexico, dating from 1821 to 1880, the value of silver extracted amounted to 4,503,291,545f., and that of gold to 247,068,930f. Since 1537 to 1880 the average annual production of gold and silver has been about 45,300,000f. An authority on the subject states that it only requires an improved method of extracting the ore to raise Mexico to the first rank of countries to which the world looks for its supply of the precious metals.

SOME LAND in the city of London has been sold at the rate of $3,300,000 an acre.

CALIFORNIA produces half the quicksilver in the world—100,222,267 pounds in the last thirty years, of which two-thirds went abroad.

M. BAVERET WATEL considers systems of irrigation as the cause of a sweeping destruction of fish. The fry go into the channels and die when the water is withdrawn suddenly.

"God Save the Queen" has been translated into all the dialects of India.

COLBURN'S BUTTE. — Thomas Moran.

THE WILD PASSES OF THE SHENANDOAH VALLEY are particularly noticeable because of the extensive vistas they lead to. This valley is quite properly called "The Garden of Virginia," since it is made up of all the features essential to the picturesque. In addition it possesses phenomena most wonderful to contemplate. Here are the celebrated Caverns of Luray and that world-renowned arch, The Natural Bridge of Virginia. When you have explored the recesses of one and crossed the other you have held closer relationship with Dame Nature than ever before.

SEPTEMBER should be called the month of many names. The Roman Senate would have given it the name of Tiberius, but that Emperor opposed it; the Emperor Domitian gave it his own name, Germanicus; the Senate under Antoninus Pius gave it that of Antoninus; Commodus gave it his surname, Herculeus; and the Emperor Tacitus his own name, Tacitus.

9th Mo. SEPTEMBER. 30 days.

Year Day	Month Day	Week Day	Moon, Wash'ton M. Time	Sun Rises	Sun Sets	Moon Rises	Moon Phase
			H. M. S.	H. M.	H. M.	H. M.	
244	1	Tu	11 59 42	5 29	6 30	10 52	
245	2	W	11 59 23	5 30	6 28	11 48	3 Q.
246	3	Th	11 59 3	5 31	6 27	morn	
247	4	Fr	11 58 44	5 32	6 25	0 42	
248	5	Sa	11 58 24	5 33	6 24	1 16	
249	6		11 58 4	5 34	6 22	2 54	
250	7	M	11 57 44	5 35	6 21	4 3	
251	8	Tu	11 57 23	5 36	6 19	sets.	N.
252	9	W	11 57 3	5 37	6 17	6 51	
253	10	Th	11 56 42	5 37	6 16	7 28	
254	11	Fr	11 56 22	5 38	6 14	8 4	
255	12	Sa	11 56 1	5 39	6 13	8 41	
256	13		11 55 40	5 40	6 11	9 20	
257	14	M	11 55 19	5 41	6 10	10 1	
258	15	Tu	11 54 58	5 42	6 8	10 46	
259	16	W	11 54 36	5 43	6 6	11 33	1 Q.
260	17	Th	11 54 15	5 44	6 5	morn.	
261	18	Fr	11 53 54	5 45	6 3	0 22	
262	19	Sa	11 53 33	5 46	6 2	1 14	
263	20		11 53 12	5 46	6 0	2 9	
264	21	M	11 52 51	5 47	5 58	3 5	
265	22	Tu	11 52 30	5 48	5 57	1 2	
266	23	W	11 52 9	5 49	5 55	5 1	
267	24	Th	11 51 48	5 50	5 53	rises.	F.
268	25	Fr	11 51 28	5 51	5 52	6 18	
269	26	Sa	11 51 7	5 52	5 50	7 25	
270	27		11 50 47	5 53	5 49	8 5	
271	28	M	11 50 27	5 54	5 47	8 50	
272	29	Tu	11 50 7	5 55	5 45	9 40	
273	30	W	11 49 48	5 56	5 44	10 35	

10th Mo. OCTOBER. 31 days.

Year Day	Month Day	Week Day	Moon. Wash'ton M. Time. H. M. S.	Sun Rises H. M.	Sun Sets H. M.	Moon Rises H. M.	Moon Phase
274	1	Th	11 49 29	5 57	5 42	11 36	3 Q.
275	2	Fr	11 49 10	5 58	5 41	morn.	
276	3	Sa	11 48 52	5 59	5 39	0 41	
277	4	Su	11 48 34	5 59	5 38	1 47	
278	5	M	11 48 16	6 0	5 36	2 55	
279	6	Tu	11 47 59	6 1	5 35	4 3	
280	7	W	11 47 42	6 2	5 33	5 9	
281	8	Th	11 47 25	6 3	5 32	sets.	N.
282	9	Fr	11 47 9	6 4	5 30	6 35	
283	10	Sa	11 46 54	6 5	5 29	7 11	
284	11	Su	11 46 39	6 6	5 27	7 55	
285	12	M	11 46 24	6 7	5 26	8 38	
286	13	Tu	11 46 10	6 8	5 24	9 25	
287	14	W	11 45 56	6 9	5 23	10 11	
288	15	Th	11 45 43	6 10	5 21	11 5	1 Q.
289	16	Fr	11 45 31	6 11	5 20	11 58	
290	17	Sa	11 45 19	6 12	5 18	morn.	
291	18	Su	11 45 8	6 13	5 17	0 53	
292	19	M	11 44 57	6 14	5 16	1 50	
293	20	Tu	11 44 47	6 15	5 14	2 47	
294	21	W	11 44 37	6 16	5 13	3 47	
295	22	Th	11 44 28	6 17	5 12	4 48	
296	23	Fr	11 44 20	6 19	5 10	rises.	F.
297	24	Sa	11 44 13	6 20	5 9	6 2	
298	25	Su	11 44 6	6 21	5 8	6 46	
299	26	M	11 44 0	6 22	5 6	7 35	
300	27	Tu	11 43 55	6 23	5 5	8 30	
301	28	W	11 43 51	6 24	5 4	9 30	
302	29	Th	11 43 47	6 25	5 3	10 33	
303	30	Fr	11 43 44	6 26	5 2	11 39	3 Q.
304	31	Sa	11 43 42	6 27	5 0	morn.	

VETA PASS.

To the civil engineer Colorado has extraordinary things to show. Her railroads, passing through canyons thousands of feet deep, or over mountain passes above the clouds, are acknowledged by all who have ever seen them to be triumphs of engineering skill that have not only never been equaled, but have never even been approached. For sharp curves and steep grades, without which a road over the mountains would be impossible, the Denver and Rio Grande railway is one of the wonders of the world. A few years ago it would have been considered madness to attempt what its daring engineers have accomplished, not in an isolated instance only, but in a score of cases where the topography of the country seemed to defy further advance. We need mention only a few instances, such as Fremont's Pass, Marshall Pass and Tennessee Pass, where the iron horse mounts to an altitude of over 10,000 feet; the Royal Gorge of the Arkansas, where the channel is so narrow and the river so rapid that genius resorted to the expedient of suspending a bridge from truss-work fastened in the walls of the canyon; and Toltec Gorge, where, after passing through a tunnel bored through the solid rock, the train moves along the brink of a

CASTLE WARTBURG.—C. Hein.

chasm 1,200 feet above Los Pinos Creek below. But more wonderful still is the Pass of La Veta, where, after making the shortest curve on any railway in the world, the train ascends the mountain side on a grade from 211 to 217 feet per mile.

A NEW adulterant of ground pepper is a finely ground preparation of the kernels of olive berries. If a sample of the suspected mixture is scattered upon a mixture of equal volumes of glycerine and water, the pepper floats upon the surface while the ground olive kernels sink.

IT WAS IN CASTLE WARTBURG, at Eisenach, that Luther found refuge after the Diet of Worms, and occupied his time with his translation of the Bible. This was in 1521-22. The castle was built about 1070, by Louis, landgrave of Thuringia, and it was the residence of his successors for nearly four centuries. The site, a wooded hill, surrounded by rocky glens, is extremely picturesque. The castle was thoroughly restored in 1847, and adorned by Moritz von Schwind with frescoes illustrative of its history. In 1867 was celebrated the eighth centenary of its foundation.

A FLIRTATION. — Rudeaux.

11th Mo.   NOVEMBER.   30 days.

Year Day	Month Da.	Week Day	Moon R. / S.		Sun R.	Sun S.	Moon Rises	Moon Phase
			H. M. S.		H. M.	H. M.	H. M.	
305	1	Su	11 43 41		6 28	4 59	0 45	
306	2	M	11 43 40		6 29	4 58	1 51	
307	3	Tu	11 43 41		6 31	4 57	2 56	
308	4	W	11 43 42		6 32	4 56	4 4	
309	5	Th	11 43 44		6 33	4 55	5 4	
310	6	Fr	11 43 47		6 34	4 54	sets. N.	
311	7	Sa	11 43 51		6 35	4 53	5 48	
312	8	Su	11 43 55		6 36	4 52	6 31	
313	9	M	11 44 1		6 37	4 51	7 16	
314	10	Tu	11 44 7		6 38	4 50	8 5	
315	11	W	11 44 14		6 39	4 49	8 55	
316	12	Th	11 44 22		6 40	4 49	9 48	
317	13	Fr	11 44 31		6 41	4 48	10 42	
318	14	Sa	11 44 40		6 43	4 47	11 37	1 Q.
319	15	Su	11 44 51		6 44	4 46	morn.	
320	16	M	11 45 2		6 45	4 45	0 33	
321	17	Tu	11 45 14		6 46	4 45	1 31	
322	18	W	11 45 27		6 47	4 44	2 31	
323	19	Th	11 45 41		6 48	4 43	3 32	
324	20	Fr	11 45 55		6 49	4 43	4 36	
325	21	Sa	11 46 10		6 50	4 42	5 42	
326	22	Su	11 46 26		6 51	4 42	rises. F.	
327	23	M	11 46 43		6 52	4 41	6 18	
328	24	Tu	11 47 1		6 53	4 41	7 18	
329	25	W	11 47 19		6 55	4 40	8 22	
330	26	Th	11 47 38		6 56	4 40	9 30	
331	27	Fr	11 47 58		6 57	4 40	10 37	
332	28	Sa	11 48 19		6 58	4 39	11 44	3 Q.
333	29	Su	11 48 40		6 59	4 39	morn	
334	30	M	11 49 2		7 0	4 39	0 49	

Petit Rocks are well-known features of the scenery near Round Island, on the Sinnemahoning, a tributary of the Susquehanna, 110 miles from Sunbury, Pa. Near here is a very beautiful waterfall, 24 feet high. Landscape artists find in Pennsylvania varied and interesting subjects for their canvas, and tourists from all over the world are delighted with the charms of nature and the perfection of modern comforts and facilities of travel in the wildest and most romantic regions.

The first coach in Scotland was brought thither in 1561, when Queen Mary came from France. It belonged to Alexander, Lord Seaton.

12th Mo.   DECEMBER.   31 days.

Year Day	Moon	Week Day	Moon's s'n 'd'time	Sun Rises		Mo'n R ses	Moon Praise
335	1	Tu	11 49 25	7 1	4 39	1 53	
336	2	W	11 49 48	7 2	4 38	2 55	
337	3	Th	11 50 12	7 2	4 38	3 57	
338	4	Fr	11 50 37	7 3	4 38	4 57	
339	5	Sa	11 51 2	7 4	4 38	5 55	
340	6	☽	11 51 28	7 5	4 38	sets. N.	
341	7	M	11 51 54	7 6	4 38	5 57	
342	8	Tu	11 52 21	7 7	4 38	6 47	
343	9	W	11 52 48	7 8	4 38	7 39	
344	10	Th	11 53 15	7 9	4 38	8 32	
345	11	Fr	11 53 43	7 9	4 38	9 27	
346	12	Sa	11 54 11	7 10	4 39	10 22	
347	13	☽	11 54 40	7 11	4 39	11 19	
348	14	M	11 55 9	7 12	4 39	morn. ↑Q.	
349	15	Tu	11 55 38	7 12	4 39	0 16	
350	16	W	11 56 7	7 13	4 40	1 15	
351	17	Th	11 56 37	7 14	4 40	2 16	
352	18	Fr	11 57 6	7 14	4 40	3 20	
353	19	Sa	11 57 36	7 15	4 41	4 25	
354	20	☽	11 58 6	7 15	4 41	5 32	
355	21	M	11 58 35	7 16	4 42	rises F.	
356	22	Tu	11 59 5	7 16	4 42	6 4	
357	23	W	11 59 35	7 17	4 43	7 12	
358	24	Th	12 0 5	7 17	4 44	8 22	
359	25	Fr	12 0 35	7 17	4 44	9 32	
360	26	Sa	12 1 5	7 18	4 45	10 40	
361	27	☽	12 1 31	7 18	4 45	11 45	
362	28	M	12 2 3	7 18	4 46	morn. 3Q.	
363	29	Tu	12 2 33	7 19	4 47	0 49	
364	30	W	12 3 2	7 19	4 48	1 51	
365	31	Th	12 3 30	7 19	4 48	2 51	

SAINT NICHOLAS, Bishop of Myra, died about A. D. 340. He is invoked as the patron of sailors, merchants, travelers and captives, and the guardian of schoolboys, girls and children. In the Greek Church he ranks immediately after the great fathers. He has been reverenced in the West of Europe since the tenth century, and became one of the favorite patron saints of Italy and Northern Europe about the beginning of the twelfth.

CHRISTMAS, as any one not acquainted with the fact might infer, is taken from the title, Christ, which was added to the name of Jesus, to express that he was the Messiah, or "The Anointed." St. Clement, the earliest father, according to St. Epiphanius, fixed the birth of Christ on the 18th of November, in the 28th year of Augustus, i. e., two years before the Christian era, as adopted in the sixth century. The date now most generally accepted is Monday, December 25, A. M. 4,004, in the year of Rome 752. The divinity of Jesus Christ was adopted by the Council of Nice in A. D. 325, by two hundred and ninety-nine bishops against eighteen.

LAS VEGAS HOT SPRINGS.

A JAUNT THROUGH NEW MEXICO reveals to the traveler a wonderful country, which the most glowing words cannot do justice to. Composed of mountain and cañon, giant forest, great falls, inexhaustible water-courses and health-giving springs, the scope for description is unlimited, but the multiplicity of phases defy our language. Through this section of our country civilization has closely followed the building of the railroad. Enterprising people have migrated into and scattered themselves over the surface, and towns have sprung up and grown as if by magic. Hotels bearing the stamp more or less distinctly of Eastern progressiveness are now seen, where formerly, if at all, log, adobe and mud structures existed. The progress made in New Mexico has excited great interest, and, combined with the natural attractions, is rapidly gaining accession from the outside world. The floating population which pours through St. Louis on its way to the Pacific are thus afforded much to delight them *en route*, and seekers after health and pleasure alight here and there with beneficial and gratifying results.

From Atchison or Kansas City, a ride of less than forty hours in luxuriant palace-cars, combining every comfort, conveys the tourist to Las Vegas Hot Springs, New Mexico, in the pine-clad foot-hills of the Spanish Range of the Rocky Mountains—a spot which seems to have been designed by Nature for the very purpose it is used. Las Vegas, meaning "the meadows," lies on a beautiful plateau comprising thirty acres or more of almost level surface. Stony cliffs tower above it several hundred feet in the air, and a splashing stream — the river Gallinas — passes through it, flowing cold and swift from the snowy peaks

of the Rockies. Here are a series of the most remarkable springs yet discovered in the land, and known to possess all the curative properties of the Arkansas Hot Springs, together with a climate dry and pure, and an electric atmosphere entirely free from malaria. A comparison of these waters with the world-renowned healing waters of Karlsbad, Germany, shows them to be almost identical in analysis.

Former visitors at "The Montezuma," the famous Las Vegas Hot Springs hotel, which was burned down last year, will be pleased to learn that a new "Montezuma" (which we illustrate) has been erected on a grander and more magnificent scale. The material is the beautiful red and white granite which forms the picturesque bluffs of the Gallinas and is so abundant at the Springs. It is situated on an elevation commanding a magnificent view of the Gallinas Cañon. It is absolutely fireproof, and everything that the former hotel contributed to the pleasure and comfort of guests has been retained, and many new improvements added. Elegant and complete accommodations for 300 guests are now provided, and invalids receive the same kindly care and have every facility for enjoying the baths as formerly.

Encouraged by the flattering patronage of past seasons, no cost has been spared to more than maintain the well-won reputation of the "Montezuma" as one of the best inns between the Missouri and the Pacific, and the railroad company to whom this building is due deserves the thanks of the public for their enterprise. The schedules of the Atchison, Topeka and Santa Fe Railroad furnish all necessary directions for reaching this resort.

A FLORIDA HUMMOCK.—J. D. Woodward.

PICCOLO.

A FLORIDA HUMMOCK is a stretch of fertile and timbered land, on which grow in luxuriant profusion oaks, magnolias and laurels, also fig, orange, lemon, and numerous other fruit trees. The flowery kingdom is represented by hundreds of varieties, making the air redolent with perfume. Springs of pure water bubble up from the soil, forming crystal basins and sparkling rills.

"EENTY, meenty, minety, mo," and "Eny, meeny, mony, mike," which children recite in some of their games and commonly considered gibberish, are in reality remnants of the language of the earliest inhabitants of the British Isles.

DRESSES in the sixteenth century were costly articles, rich in gold embroidery and valuable material, as the relics that have come down to us still show. Much art was expended on embroidery and delicate needlework, in which the skill of the worker was generally in advance of the taste of the designer. It may be of interest to know that Queen Elizabeth possessed a dress embroidered in a pattern of eyes and ears, and a yet more uncomfortable garment was manufactured at a little later date, viz., a robe worked in eyelet-holes, with the needle with which each hole was worked hanging to it by a thread. Perhaps our lady friends can revive the style?

PICCOLA.

IN SOME OF THE LATIN tongues of Southern Europe — the Italian especially, and the French in a similar degree, though in different modes — the terminations of words have great influence in explaining their meaning, and those of proper names actually determine their sex, as do the French prefixes "Le" and "La" tell to a certainty whether a man or a woman is being spoken of. In Italian the most marked difference is to be found in the "o" or "a" of the termination. In the pictures "Piccolo" and "Piccola" we have illustrations of this difference, equally evident in the names and the personalities. They are both Italian children, and greatly illustrate the brunette and dark-eyed beauty of the land of poetry and song.

AN EXCHANGE calls attention to the immense utility of the cocoanut as food rations, and the valuable qualities which it has for supplying nutrition. Two men once drifted in a whale boat to an island, where they remained for seven years before they were taken off. They had no food beyond a chance flying fish and cocoanuts, and yet when they were rescued they were in excellent condition and had gained considerably in weight.

ENGLAND has $10,000,000,000 invested abroad.

PRIZE RECIPES.

MAY'S CRULLARS.- 2 cups sugar, 2 eggs, 1 cup buttermilk (or sweet), 1 teaspoonful soda, 2 teaspoonfuls cream tartar, 6 tablespoonfuls melted lard, salt and nutmeg. Not too stiff.

COTTAGE PUDDING.- 1 pint flour, 1 teacup milk, 1 egg, ½ teacup sugar, 1 teaspoonful soda, 2 teaspoonfuls cream tartar, salt. Either soft or hard sauce.

SPONGE CAKE.—8 eggs, 1 pound sugar, ½ pound flour, the grated rind of 1 lemon, or juice of ½ lemon and salt.

BROWN BREAD.—1 cup sponge, 1 cup corn meal, 2 cups coarse flour, 2 tablespoonfuls molasses, a little salt ; wet with milk. Stir stiff as you can. Let stand in pans till raised.

TO CAN FRUIT.- 1 teacup sugar to 1 quart fruit, and *very* little water.

SWEET PICKLING.—3 pounds of sugar to 7 pounds of fruit and 1 pint of vinegar ; cinnamon ; and stick 3 cloves in each fruit.

MARBLE CAKE—*Light Part.*-1 cup white sugar, ½ cup butter, ½ cup milk, whites of 3 eggs, 2 cups flour, ½ teaspoonful baking powder. *Dark Part.*—½ cup brown sugar, ¼ cup butter, ½ cup molasses, ¼ cup milk, yolks of 3 eggs, 1 nutmeg, 2 cups flour, 2 teaspoonfuls cinnamon, 1 or 2 teaspoonfuls allspice, ½ teaspoonful baking powder, salt.

CORN BREAD.—1 quart Indian meal, 3 handfuls flour, 3 teacups sour milk, 1 teacup sugar or molasses or half and half, butter size of egg, 2 eggs, 1 teaspoonful soda.

ROLL JELLY CAKE.—4 eggs, 1 cup sugar, 1 cup flour, 1 teaspoonful baking powder, salt. Bake in quick oven. Spread jelly on bottom of cake while hot ; then roll.

HOUSEHOLD MEASURES.—1 pound flour=1 quart ; 18 oz. meal=1 quart ; 1 pound butter=1 pint ; 1 pound sugar=1 pint ; 10 eggs=1 pound.

STRAWBERRY ICE CREAM.—Rub 1 pint of strawberries through sieve, add 1 pint of cream, 4 oz. powdered sugar, and freeze it.

SUET PUDDING.- 1 cup chopped suet, 1 cup raisins, 1 cup molasses, 1 cup milk, 3 cups flour, 1 teaspoonful of baking powder, salt. Boil 3 hours.

GRANDMA'S DOUGHNUTS.-6 cups dough, 1 cup sugar, 3 or 4 tablespoonfuls melted lard, 1 egg, ½ teaspoonful of baking powder ; salt and cinnamon. After cutting let stand for an hour before frying.

QUICK BISCUIT.—3 cups flour, 1 cup milk, 1 tablespoonful of butter, 2 teaspoonfuls baking powder ; salt.

GINGER SNAPS.—2 cups molasses, 1 cup shortening, 1 teaspoonful of baking powder, 1 teaspoonful ginger ; salt.

ANGEL CAKE.—1½ teacups pulverized sugar, 1 teacup flour, whites 10 eggs ; ½ teaspoonful baking powder ; salt and flavor.

FRUIT CAKE. -2 cups butter, 3 cups sugar, 3½ cups flour, 8 eggs, 1 pound raisins, 1 pound citron. 1 teaspoonful cloves, 1 teaspoonful cinnamon, 1 nutmeg or a little mace, 1 gill brandy or milk.

CORN CAKE.—½ cup sugar, 1 tablespoonful butter, 4 eggs. 1 teaspoonful baking powder. 1 cup flour, 1 quart milk. Thicken with Indian meal.

PUFF OVERS.—2 cups sweet milk, 2 cups flour, 2 eggs, salt. Bake 15 minutes in quick oven.

EUREKA POUND CAKE.- 4 cups flour, 4 cups sugar, 2 cups butter, 6 eggs, 1 cup milk, 2 teaspoonfuls baking powder.

BERMUDA CAKE.—2 cups molasses, 1 cup sugar, 1 cup butter, 1 cup milk, ¾ pound raisins, ¼ pound citron, 1 nutmeg, 8 eggs, 4 cups flour. cloves and cinnamon.

RICE PUDDING WITHOUT EGGS.—2 quarts milk, 1½ to 2 teacups rice, 1 teacup sugar, 1 teacup raisins, butter size of an egg, nutmeg. Bake 2 hours.

SUGAR COOKIES.--2 cups sugar, 1 cup butter, 1 cup milk, 2 eggs, 1 teaspoonful baking powder, 1 nutmeg, flour to roll soft, salt.

CORN FRITTERS.—1 dozen ears sweet corn, 2 tablespoonfuls flour, 3 eggs, salt, little milk. Fry in sweet lard.

ORANGE FOR LAYER CAKE.--4 oranges, grated; whites of 2 eggs, 2 tablespoonfuls water, 1½ cups sugar. Boil eggs. sugar and water together 15 minutes ; then mix with orange ; then spread.

RIPE TOMATO PICKLES.—2 gallons tomatoes, peeled, not sliced ; 1 pint vinegar, 2 pounds sugar. Mace. nutmeg and cinnamon to taste,

TO MAKE COFFEE- *Boiled.*-½ pint ground coffee, 1 quart boiling water, white of one egg and shell of same.

JELLY WATER. 1 large teaspoonful currant or cranberry jelly, 1 goblet ice water. Beat up well for fever patient. Wild cherry or blackberry jelly is excellent, prepared same, for summer complaint.

WINE WHEY.—1 pint boiling milk, 1 large glass pale wine, poured in when milk is hot. Boil up once ; remove from fire and let cool. Do not stir after wine is in. When curd forms, draw off whey and sweeten.

TO WASH DOUBTFUL CALICOES.—Put teaspoonful of sugar of lead in pail of water ; soak 15 minutes before washing.

ANTIDOTE TO POISON.- For *any* poison swallow instantly a glass of cold water with teaspoonful salt and teaspoonful ground mustard stirred in. This is a speedy emetic. When it has acted swallow whites of two raw eggs.

COLOGNE WATER.—1 drachm oil lavender, 1 drachm oil bergamot, 2 drachms oil lemon. 2 drachms oil rosemary, 50 drops tincture musk. 8 drops oil cinnamon, 8 drops oil cloves, 1 pint alcohol.

THE BLADE ANNUAL

—AND

HISTORY OF CLOUD COUNTY.

By J. M. HAGAMAN.

As time widens the distance between the past and present, so in proportion does the past become of interest to those now living. We look upon scenes of to-day with cold indifference that a generation hence will ransack the records to find the smallest information concerning. So when the stiring scenes on this border were being enacted; when the buffalo covered every hill and valley; the brutal savage, with tomahawk and scalping knife, menaced the few and scattered settlers, many things occurred that were deemed by them of but passing moment, that would be read by strangers hence, with quickening interest. In the excitement of battle the expiring words of a comrade "tell my mother I died a soldier's death" is scarcely more than heard by his brother soldier, but as time rolls on,—an age has past—and the whispered words of the dying youth have echoed among hills and valleys around the earth. And very much like this is there in the experience of the frontiersman. He will hear of a massacre where whole families have been murdered by the savages, and so little thought does he take of those to come after him that he does not even jot down the date where it occurred! Of the present he cares something, of the future, nothing. "Let the 'future' take care of itself," is his motto. For this neglect many important events of early life on this border will remain untold; or will be indifferently told; and many others will be forever mute for another reason,—there are none but the actors to tell them. They are not egotists and will not therefore speak.

Our first inquiry is "When and where was the first settlement made?

Avoiding debatable ground as much as possible, we will speak of "permanent settlement." Hunters and trappers; claim takers without settlement,—have, in my judgment, no right to this honor That rests, or should rest, upon those who settled and stayed here, through

"thick and thin:" in spite of scalping Indians, drouth and grasshoppers. The men, their wives and families who did this, were those who established their homes on Elm Creek, July 15th 1860.[*] Attemps at settlement were made in the spring of this year at Elk Creek, Lake Sibley, Wolf Cree and Elm Creek, but all of these were abandoned by those who made them, the first and last being the only ones that can, with propriety, be said to have been continuous. For during a portion of the month of August the only persons living in the county were the residents of Elm Creek.

This was the "great famine year" so heralded over the world, the "poor settlers being driven from starvatiton to the eating of rats! [+] About the first of May a drouth set in which lasted till the last week in July, when copious showers fell. During the intervening period there was no rain and sod corn planted in May and June did not sprout until the July rains. And yet in the creek and river bottoms in the county grass was growing luxuriantly, trees were robed in brightest green and the black walnut was loaded with fruit; along the numerous creeks gooseberry bushes bent under their ripened fruit, while the wild grape hung in festoons from the treetops and spread far and wide over the timberless river bottoms. Surely all these could not have been without seasonable rains?

But the uplands were in a melancholly contrast with the scenery just described. Here was seen, in the seared grass and

---

[*] J. M. Hagaman, wife and one child; J. M Thorp, wife and six children; August Feaskle, wife and one child.

[+] This story started in this way: Samuel C. Chester (resides now on Peach Creek) and one or two other parties, out of a feeling of curiosity, killed some wood rats and ate them. At the time they had plenty of game, and a day's drive would take them to the buffalo. But there happened to be a gentleman present who saw in it a chance for a sensation and he improved it. He went east and told the story with much pathos and secured many a two dollars for himself and fifty cents for the "Kansas sufferers."

cracked earth, the too convincing evidence of protracted drouth. Yet the true pioneer was undismayed by this repulsive condition of the uplands,—there was enough of the valley lands to maintain a large population, and whether these would do for farming purposes or not "he would *stay* and make the most of it." *

On the hills grazed millions of the noble bison and in the slender timber lines along the numerous streams hovered innumerable flocks of wild turkeys. The elk, the deer, the antelope, the grey wolf and the coyote, skipped and played, fed and hunted on the broad prairies and in the timber; an occasional flock of grouse were startled from the prairies, fish in abundance were found in the Republican river, and along its banks, and likewise its numerous tributaries, otters, and coons hunted the finny tribe and the sagacious beaver felled trees and fed upon the bark of the limbs, built dams across the streamlets, to conceal the entrances to their houses, and sported in the dammed up waters. What a paradise was this for the hunter! What a magnificent country in which to establish a home! It was no doubt true that occasionally the clouds would fail to sufficiently condense to precipitate rain, but the splendid growth of timber, of shrubbery, of the sunflower on the highest of lands all told quite truley that seasonable rains were necessary to produce them.

"Tickle the earth and she smiles a crop" is as old a saying as Egypt is old, but it was as true of this county during the first seven years of its settlement as ever it was of that "grainery of the world" in the days of the banished Joseph.

The spring of 1861 opened out with the brightest of prospects for a good crop season. The winter had witnessed a two feet fall of snow, and the last of February warm rain began to fall, the snow soon departed, the frost left the ground and the 5th of March the cattle of the settlers fed upon the young and tender grass to the satisfying of their appetites. Early in April the soil was prepared for wheat and by the 10th that cereal was sown for the first time in the Republican Valley. It brought forth abundant grain 30 bushels to the acre being the actual yield, and of the very best quality. As soon as practicable the virgin prairie, that had never before in the myriads of ages past, been touched by the hand of cultivation, was

turned over and in its bosom was deposited the germ of the future corn crop. Potatoes, turnips, and the usual "garden truck" of eastern civilization received proper attention, and in all was there a bounteous yield, so that the autumn of 1861 found our infant colony with enough and to spare of the most essential of the products of the soil.

But now that they have raised corn and wheat whither will they go to grind it? Council Grove, 90 miles, Table Rock, 110 miles, were the nearest mills and to the first they went with their wheat and corn. Tedious trips were these in these early days when roads were almost unknown and bridges there were none.

Now that they have a crop can they market it? No! Not a dollar's worth of any produce did a man of this settlement sell in Cloud (Shirley) county for the first three years of its settlement. They sold, or rather bartered in distant towns for goods they had to have, but the prices of the goods were very high and the price of their products very low. We will mention one case as an illustration of this "dicker." Stopping at Marysville on their return from one of these trips to mill, the party of three exchanged some flour for goods. Among the articles exchanged for was a pair of "geot kip boots," as the german Jew called them, and if he had just added "good for nothing," he would have told, probably, more truth han he had previously told for a month. He put them on and went on a buffalo hunt and the fourth day he was wearing moccasins cut from the skin off the knees of a buffalo! Lucky too, in getting the buffalo, for the boots had teetotally failed—the insoles being made of paper! Three dollars per hundred was the price agreed to be paid for the flour, but which in fact, did not amount to the half of that in value. And yet we hold to day, in very high regard, that German Jew, for we had to have some goods, at whatever sacrifice, and he was the only man in the hundred miles of travel we could get any offer at all for our flour and we had no other way of getting them.

THE FIRST WINTER IN SHIRLEY.

How did the colonists spend their first winter, might be a matter of interest to the reader. It is not to be supposed they imitated their eastern friends and spent it in going to balls, and parties, and religious and other assemblies, for their condition and numbers would not imply this, but they enjoyed themselves, nevertheless. In a disaster a sea, when the wild waves dash furiously

* The early settlers were very much divided in opinion as to the value of the uplands for agricultural purposes, the majority insisting that they would do for grazing, while others believed they would be for all purposes as valuable as the bottom lands. H.

against the ship's sides and she creaks and groans in every joint, and fear is prevalent among the passengers that each succeeding wave will swamp the vessel, all thought of caste, of pre-eminence by birth or wealth is abandoned and all become as common people. A brotherly and sisterly feeling prevails friendly feeling, as of one kindred, flesh and blood. Not unlike this was the feeling that animated the pioneers of this county. Cut off from the world, they had to rely upon their own resources, and the meagre means they commanded for their recreation, pleasure and pastime, and, tho strange it may seem, of these they were never in want. With that degree of caution that comes of necessity they secured during the previous autumn enough of the "staff of life" to carry them through a long winter, for that having been reared in the north, were they used to. Game was plenty and, skilled in hunting and markmanship, no difficulty was experienced in procuring it. Trapping the beaver and otter offered other means of enjoyment and which also was a resource of revenue. But the principal source of enjoyment was the neighborly feeling that brought those hardy pioneers often together in social circles. Scarcely a night passed during the first winter without the little group of pioneers meeting together at some neighbor's house and spending the evening at cards, followed by those refreshments the wild condition of the county afforded conversing upon the topics of the times the prospect of civil war and the future of this country. No pen need portray the hardships of this first winter of this colony in Shirley for comparatively few in the east, fared as well, while many thousands fared worse, "It was the happiest period of my life," have they been individually heard to say.

CHAPTER II.

IMMENSITY OF THE BUFFALO.

I do not suppose it possible for me to satisfactorily convey to the minds of those who never saw any of the vast herds of buffalo that once roamed over the plains of Kansas, of the immense number of those wild cattle that existed twenty-four years ago. Estimates of ten millions have been regarded by many whose judgements are worthy of consideration as too high, while others having experience among them have put the figures much higher. The writer believes his opportunities for *guessing* were quite as good as any person's, if not better He viewed the vast herds as they passed South in the Fall and North in the Spring in the years 1861, 1862, and 1863, and before the fearful decimation of their numbers had begun, and he unhesitatingly puts it at twice ten millions, and believes it to be much higher still than that. Let us make a little calculation: On September 8, 1860, the line of march of the buffalo extended from Elm Creek on the East to Randall, in Jewell county, on the West, a distance of thirty miles. If, now they walk twenty feet apart for that distance and each line passes a given point once a minute for 24 hours there would pass in one minute 7,920; in one hour 475,200 and in twenty four hours 11,404,800.

But this calculation presumes what did not exist. It is based on the assumption that the buffalo moved regularly which was far from being the case. On the contrary their movements were spasmodic. A great rush of hundreds of thousands, blocking the prairie as far as the eye could penetrate, and then there would be a lull for hours, in which a few hundreds of thousands would pass on, and then another rush, as intense and numerous as before. This is kept up for a whole *month* and then for four or five months more stragglers, from single ones to thousands, pass South over this thirty mile strip, and West and East of it. The writer having hunted and camped for four weeks in the Autumn of 1860 on this range (so called from its being the territory on which the buffalo fed and traveled)had an excellent opportunity of judging of the enormous number of buffalo that existed. Not only did they pass by daylight but in the night also. Often has his camp been aroused by the deafening clatter of hoofs and the heavy intonations of bellowing bulls. So impressed was he with the greatness of their number that he would not feel justified in disputing a person's statement, who had had a reasonable opportunity of judging, should he put them as high, or even higher than fifty million!

As matter of history we may state that the early settler regarded the killing of a buffalo about as much of a fete as the killing of a gray squirrel in New York state when they sported in every town. Thousands upon thousands were shot for mere sport or through mere wantonness, and left to rot on the prairie.

Of all that vast army of buffalo that roamed at will over the vast prairies lying between the Great Slave Lake, in British America on the north, and Red river, in Texas, on the south what is left of them: *A few stragglers* in the head waters of the Missouri, and the Dominion of Canada, are to be found'

The merciless rifle of the huntsman has done its fearful work and this famous beast is nearly extict. A few years hence there will be none—all will be gone. For a few years a few specimens will be kept in their purity; but 'his,like all else, will come to an end, and the noble race is gone for all time to come.

Much has been written of the buffalo that was not true,—writ'en by writers who had more love for the marvelous then they had for the truth.

The buffalo in health and strength was a coward except with his own kind. From the sight of a man standing erect he would flee. The sudden appearance of a wolf would often startle them for many miles and they would run away with all their power. Yet we have crawled on the ground in full view of thousands, and to within a few rods of them without starting them. Why was this? The crawling object was not to them a man but let him arise to his feet and instantly they knew him to be their deadly foe. From the scent of a man they invariably fled. Thus proving that their sense of smell was more reliable than their sight. Rarely did a hunter approach in gun shot of a buffalo from the windward side.

THE BUFFALO NEARLY EXTINCT.

In glancing back at the ages past and viewing the world as revealed by the pen of the historian, the rocks and fossils, one stands awe stricken as he gazes upon the myriads of races of animals that have lived and died—leaving nothing behind them but their foot prints in the clay or fragments of their frame work in marshy lands. They have perished through the law of evolution, of the "survival of the fittest," and the buffalo are going—are nearly gone—the same way. A generation hence and not *one* full blood, on the globe! Like his predecessor, the giant mastodon, he is too cumbrous for the time and he "must go" and make room for a better, more useful race of animals.

Much has been written about the "superior value" of the buffalo over the domestic ox for food, but this is simply absurd True, to a person who has a peculiar relish for *sinew*, the buffalo would prove a dainty dish, but as most people prefer 'flesh' to leather 'meat' to hempen cords, the ox would be far the most valuable to them. A century or two of domestication might make the buffalo the equal of the domestic ox, but why take the trouble, he could never be superior? The "hump," which has been extolled so much is, indeed, the least valuable for food. It is coarse grained and tough, far inferior to the ham.

However, the buffalo subserved a good purpose to the early settler. His flesh was eatable, his hide served for bedding and moccasins. His tallow took the place of lard in the culinary department. Without him the settlers could not have survived on this border in the early days, and for this reason alone we tender him our "homage and our thanks."

Noble beast ! with all of your imperfections, you have subserved a good purpose, and as you are no longer needed, pass on and make room for your superiors ! So has cold, selfish, heartless nature bid myriads of other races go, and it is no worse for you than they. The time is not far distant when the last crack of the hunter's rifle will be heard by you, the tales of the sportsman will keep alive for awhile your sad memories, but that too, will cease and you will be forgotten.

Thus will end the career of one of the most important of the brute races. First found in the East, gradually has he been driven Westward, like his companion, the red man, to perish, finally, in the rocky mountains.

CHAPTER III.

THE GOODS AND ILLS OF FRONTIER LIFE.

During the year of 1861 several additions were made to the settlers by the arrival of immigrants, but the repeated threatened out breaks of Indians discouraged many from coming and caused some settlers to leave.

The spring of 1862 opened up less favorably than did that of 1861, but undismayed by this and the bad reports from 1860, our colonists went bravely to work and planted as though the adaptability of the country to farming had been demonstrated, and success again crowned their efforts. Timely rains fell and the produce yield was large.

One of the great inconveniences the settler was compelled to undergo was that of seeking a distant market for his products. It has been the case in settlement of most of the western states that the incoming immigration would buy, a portion at least, of his surplus produce, but not so here. The arrivals were so few and their demands so trifling that the producer was scarcely benefitted by them, so he had to seek a market elsewhere. Having this object in view several settlers loaded their wagons with corn, butter, and sorghum and started in June for Fort Kearney, one hundred and forty miles distant, in Nebraska. The bridges on the old Fort Rilley and Fort Kearney road having been washed away during the unprecedented high waters of 1861, a new road had to be chosen. Accordingly two parties set out, one from Clifton and the other from Elm creek, and joining at Elk they traveled northwesterly over the divide (high) of ground between two streams between Elk and Salt creeks to the head of the latter stream, and then continued this course until they reached the little Blue river, along which ran the great overland route to Colorado, Utah and California. Here they found a hard beaten road more than a hundred feet wide and on either side of it lay, quite plentifully, skeletons and carcasses in various stages of decomposition, of oxen and mules, which had been driven to death or starved.

Their corn netted them in Fort Kearney 92½ cents per bushel; sorghum $1.00 per gallon and butter 50 cents per pound. Payments were made in greenbacks.

This was a pleasant and profitable trip, made in the pleasantest time in the year. A few buffaloes were seen on the head of Rose creek and one of the party having been sent to kill one, did so. Badly wounding him at the first shot, he conceived the idea of driving him to camp. It did not work well. The buffalo would drive for a few rods and then he would turn on his pursuer and drive him! This was repeated several times, the buffalo gaining each time, so that at the end of a half hour he was farther from camp than when the driving began! Night approaching the hunter finished him with another shot, and, like hundreds of thousands of others of his race, he was left to rot.

From Salt creek to the Blue river, thirty miles, there was not a settler and only ranches along the great highway up that river. *

These were usually six to twelve miles apart.

How often in the history of a new country infested with Indians the inhabitants dream of safety when the savage was lurking in the bushes with deadly intent! Thus thought this little band as they were eating their breakfasts on the head of Salt creek on their return. Not one but what would have bet his outfit that there was not an Indian nearer then fifty miles and those the friendly Otoes, when, of a sudden, eight Cheyennes in full war costume rode up on a hill right close to the camp! They were armed to the teeth, having bows and arrows, each a revolver and rifle, tomyhawk and knife. Had they been disposed they could have shot every man of our company before their presence was suspected. Two years later that would have been their fate. They

* A place for feeding stock, and the keepers are called "ranchmen." The usual charge this side of Fort Kearney was 25 cents a team.

were friendly now, but two years afterwards this and another band, murdered thirty-five ranchmen on the Little Blue where our party had been.

They, and several hundred others, had been pursuing the Otoe Indians with the determination of slaying them. In this they were foiled by the vigilance of the pursued.

The company hastened home, knowing full well that other bands had appeared on the border.

The settlements were in commotion, many settlers having fled the country, some of them never to return. As they went, pitiful tales they told of Indian outrages, but none however, beyond petty thieving, were committed.

Late in the summer of this year a disgraceful outrage was committed against a family named Conkling. The family consisted of Peter and Charles, men grown, and two sisters, Roxy and Ann and a small child. Stories were circulated against the boys that they had secreted stolen horses and on the strength of this report a mob from Washington and Clay counties tore down their house and turned the two women and child out of doors. The boys made their escape and a week or two afterwards a friendly neighbor, at the risk of his life, moved them to Paola.

The charge of stealing, or secreting stolen horses, was made by an enemy and was without foundation in fact.

They were industrious and frugal, and had opened up quite a farm. The whole proceeding against them was a villianous outrage, and its originators deserved condign punishment.

Another shameful outrage was perpetrated in May by the "wild" Indians. Mrs. Ann Wilson (Ann Chagron) was returning home from Elm Creek where she had been visiting a family, her husband, George, was working for. He accompanied her across the river and had left her but a short time when six Indians rode up on horse back, and five dismounting, outraged her person. Their treatment of her and her babe was of the most brutal kind. Seizing the child they gave it a fling and sent it rolling over the prairie. Laying hold of her they threw her to the ground and poised a lance over her throat threatening death if she did not cease calling for help. Having accomplished their diabolical purpose they rode off and she made her way, as best she could, to the nearest settlement and told of her wrong. There being but one or two horses in the country at this time, pursuit was not attempted and the outrage went unavenged.

Several outrages were perpetrated

this year by the "wild" Indians upon buffalo hunters, one of which we will relate.

In December two Elm Creek settlers went on a buffalo hunt intending to be gone two weeks. They were well provided with food for themselves and team of cattle and a horse. The second day out, and shortly after crossing Solomon river, a party of Cheyenne Indians, numbering forty, rode down upon them with their fleet-footed ponies, as fast as they could ride, and shouting their dreaded war whoop as they rode. They were in full war paint and armed to the teeth, and as they rode up to the lone men everyone of them levelled some weapon of death and pointed it at them, and, with that devilish look that only the brutal, heartless savage can give, they held them for some moments as if intending to do the work of death. They found in the men not the arrant cowards they had expected—who would run and leave them in possession of their cattle, horse and goods. So they contented themselves with taking, quite liberally of their stock of provisions—so "liberally" there was scarcely any left! The men returned home, not caring to venture their lives further among a lot of cut throat savages.

1863. This year opened up auspiciously for farming and continued favorable to the close of the season. Timely rains fell and crops were good, a few immigrants arrived, but the periodical "Indian scare" caused about as many to leave as came. On the range several outrages upon hunters were committed by the lawless bands of Indians that hovered near the border, constantly bent on robbery and murder.

Early in January of this year an outrage was perpetrated on a party of three hunters on Limestone that deserves to be related. The hunters had secured all the buffalo they wanted and were on their return, when about ten in the morning of a bright, clear, warm day, some thirty or forty of the most fiendish looking savages rode down upon them threatening them with instant death. They were relieved of their bread, coffee, tea and most of their ammunition, and after much rough treatment were permitted to go on their way home.

This outrage was made known to Lieut. ——— in command of Co. I of the 9th Kansas Cavalry, who was in camp with his company at Clifton. He was stationed there to protect the border from Indian depredations and it will not be uninteresting to the reader to know how he performed his work. On receiving notice of the outrage he ordered his command to prepare rations for themselves and horses for *three* days and having done this they began their march. The first day they

reached Elm Creek and the next day they came within five miles of the place where the outrage occurred and now as they had but one days rations left, and it would require two days to get back to camp, the Lieutenant ordered them to "about face" and they returned!

That was a fare sample of the protection given the frontiers during the dark period of its history. Thousands of men idled away their time in camp that had better been spent on the march—better for the health of the men and better for the country. The reason this was not done was because the officers preferred ease and good pay to the hardships of the march and no increase of pay. The writer has nothing but supreme contempt for nine tenths of the "soldiering" against Indians. It has mainly been "shamming" war.

The first election held in this county was held this year. The whole county was one precinct and the voting place was at the house of J. M. Hagaman, on Elm creek. At this time it was supposed by the people of Washington and Shirley counties that the county was attached to Washington county as a municipal township and the election was held and the vote cast under that belief for Washinton county candidates. But Shirley was not so attached, however, and the votes cast here were all illegal. By some strange oversight when the county lines were formed, in 1859—60, the county was attached to Marshall for Judicial purposes, making it a municipal township at that county, thus skipping over Washington county. The votes were supposed to be legal and were counted and elected Rufus Darby, straight Republican, over J. G. Hollenburg, mixed Republican and Democrat, by two votes. J. M. Hagaman, of this county, was elected assessor. Twenty five votes were polled, twenty three being republican and two democratic. The jurisdiction of the assessor comprised Washington, Republic and Shirley, and it required seven hundred and fifty miles travel to do the assessing. The taxable property amounted to less than one hundred thousand dollars. Sixteen days work was charged against the county at two dollars and fifty cents per day, and as there was no money to pay this with, the orders had to be hawked around the county and sold for fifty cents on the dollar.

During the session of the legislature following, E. C. Manning, Senator from the district embraced in Marshall, Riley, Clay, Washington, Republic and Shirley, discovered the error and had an act passed extending the lines of Washington county over Shirley and Republic, reserving the right to each to organize when it chose to and sever its connection with Washington.

1864. The forepart of the winter of 1863-4 was quite severe. On the third day of December a snow storm set in and lasted for three days, in which nearly a foot of snow fell. The weather moderated towards the close of the month and the snow melted. Ice in the river was scarcely more than six inches thick at any time. Hunting on the range had become so hazzardous it was not indulged in to any great extent. Yet there was no difficulty in picking up now and then a straggling buffalo.

The spring of this year was ushered in with assuring rains and a fair crop season seemed in prospect which was realized.

In August came the "annual scare" and settlers fled from White Rock and Republic county, going as far East as Clay Center. The danger of an Indian massacre was imminent, and doubtless would have occurred had not the people in the most exposed districts left. Those on the Little Blue, in Nebraska, who heeded not the repeated warnings, paid the penalty of death for their rashness. Hunters who were caught on the buffalo range were robbed and in some cases murdered. It required more than ordinary courage to remain on the border, yet a few families remained. Nearly all business was neglected and the principal talk was about Indians and of a probable raid by them on the the settlements. The excitement was greatly increased by a report brought in by Wm. Chapanskie, who with a little son had started for Fort Kearney with a load of produce, of the destruction of ranches on the Little Blue river. Mr. C. found the ranch at the junction of our road with the Great California road, smoldering in its ruins. He drove on to the next ranch and found it also in ruins, and still pushing forward, from the hight of ground that gave him a view of the country for many miles ahead he could see no building standing and he retraced his steps and hurried home.

The raid had been made and the deadly work done. Between Fort Kearney and the junction ranch over thirty five persons had been murdered, and several woman carried into captivity to be used to gratify the lust of the dirty, lousy, villianous savage. A score of ranches had been burned and a large amount of stock and other property carried off. A Mr. Kelly was the first man to suffer death. A squad of Indians, in the garb of friendship, called him out of his house and while engaged in a conversation with them, one slyly sent an arrow into his heart. He staggered back into the house and expired. The young woman to whom he was shortly to be married was carried into captivity. One family by the name of Eubank were all murdered but one woman who was carried off. A child was put into an oven and baked. Another while taking refuge in a well, was shot. A half dozen men and a woman in Pawnee ranch barricaded their windows and doors and otherwise showed fight and were saved.

As may be expected the uncolored tale of Mr. Chapanskie fed the embers of fear and it became a livid flame. The country suddenly became nearly depopulated. Wives, with tears in their eyes, begged their husbands, "for God's sake and the sake of their children, to leave the 'God cursed' Indian pestered country.

Still, some refused to go, being determined to maintain their ground or die in the attemp .

At length a feeling was aroused that culminated in a determination on the part of the settlers to know the worst, and a party of about forty men well armed and under the command of captain Schooley started for the plains. Reaching the mouth of White Rock creek the captain called a council and a majority elected to return. A squad of a dozen, however, refused to obey orders to retreat, and headed by G. D. Brooks and J. M. Hagaman they scoured the country up White Rock, and thence going south to the head of Limestone, followed down it to its mouth and returned home. Indians had been there in numbers, but somethime previous. They left, undoubtedly, immediately after the raid on the Little Blue.

So, again, after the danger was past, the settlers had taken measures for their safety.

For Mr. Schooley we will say that he was a consumate coward and absolutely unfit for the position of captain to which he had been chosen of a camping in the 17th Kansas State Militia. When he was about to leave on this expedition some of the wives of the men who went were much excited lest their husbands would get killed, but the captain's wife very confidently advised them that "they need not fear as the captain would not take them where there was any danger." She seemed to know him.

On the return of the twelve and the assurance they brought, quiet was restored and the settlers mostly returned to their homes. To them is due the credit of saving the settlements from abandonment and none will withhold it from them.*

* The following are the names of the party: J. M Hagaman, 1st Lieut : Daniel Myers, 2nd Lieut. : Samuel C. Chester, 3rd Lieut and G. D. Brooks Ensign officer of Co. Co., 17th Regiment Kansas Volunteer Militia: Civilians, W. M. Wilcox, Richard Coughlen, Charles Huntress and James C. Neely.

Do not remember names of the others. H

The eastern line of march of the buffalo, this year, when on their periodical journey north, passed along White's Creek. A few stragglers were seen farther east. About the first of James' party of hunters from Elm Creek left home in the forenoon with ox teams and just before sundown they came to a herd and killed nine in less than fifteen minutes after the first shot was fired. Forty or fifty were slaughtered on this hunt and a bufalo calf caught.

The rain-fall had decreased each year since 1831, the fall being about 34 inches that year, 34 inches in 1862, 32 inches in 1863 and 30 inches in 1854. The rain this year, limited tho' it was, however, came timely and a fair crop of corn was raised. Wheat was remarkable for the amount of smut it contained. One tenth was smut! We do not believe the like was ever before witnessed. The cause of it is unexplainable. The next year's crop raised from this seed contained no more smut than usual. The writer carfully selected fifty heads with smut kearnels in each and sowed it by itself and the result was not a kearnel of smut in it. This and the general result alluded to, would seem to strongly disprove the theory that smut produces smut.

There was now quite a number of children of school age in the Elm Creek settlement and the people began to consider the necessity of having a school. Accordingly school district No. 4 was organized, with John M. Thorp, Director, James M. Hagaman Clerk, and Zachariah Swearingen Treasurer. Miss Rosella S. Honey was employed as teacher.* The first term was held in a house furnished free by J. M. Hagaman, and during this term a log school house was erected. It was placed on the S. E. corner of Sec. 34, half a mile from Elm Creek on the parallel road. Miss Honey opened school about July first and the term ended September 30. She was again employed and taught the winter school. April 13, she made the following report to the school board, omitting formalities:

Males enrolled, 12; females, 9—total 21. Subjects of study: Alphabet, spelling, reading, penmanship, mental arithmetic, written arithmatic, geography and English Grammar. Text books, Sander's speller, definer and analyzer. Readers, Wilson's and Sanders'. Arithmatics. Thompson's First Lessons. Thompson's and Ray's Pratical. Geographies, Cornell's; Grammar, Butler's. The report was made April 13, 1865, and signed.

ROSELLA S. HONEY.

* The superintendent of Washington county, organized this district. At the time there were but three districts in that county and as Shirley was then a township of Washington, the regular order of numbering made this district No. 4.

i. T. Goodnow was State Superintendent and visited this district and lectured in the autumn of 1864 on the advantages of education. The lecture was delivered in the dwelling house of J. M. Hagaman and there were about twenty persons present. It was now the duty of the State Superintendent to recommend school books, and Mr. Goodnow recommended the Bible as the best moral instructor. Whether Miss Honey read it or not in school the writer does not remember.

There has been some controversy as to who preached the first sermon in this county and the writer is unable to settle it to his satisfaction. The honor, —or otherwise as the case may be, rests with Rev. R. P. West and ——Malat. The former preached here in October 1863, but we think he was preceded by the latter some months. Mr. Malat was sent here as a Missionary! After two years of faithful service, but without any appreciable effect, he became discouraged, shook the dust of Shirley County from his feet and sadly remarked that the Elm Creekers "might go to hell for aught he cared, as his preaching had no effect upon them!" They did not go, however, which fact was possibly due to the kindness of the Rev. Marks, from Rose Creek, Nebraska, who took pity on them and "preached" them one sermon. This gentleman possessed a stentorian voice, and for two hours made the "shakes" on the roof of the writers' house quiver while he attempted to prove there was and could not be, an Infidel! The hugeness of this joke will appear when we inform our readers that the writer's views on the Bible and religion were precisely the same then as they are now. Mr. Marks was a gentleman and very tolerant of other people's views. He never again preached on Elm Creek. Mr. West preached occasionally afterwards.

The winter of 1864-5 was remarkable for the evenness and mildness of the temperature. The river closed early, the ice formed being about a foot thick and remained that way until after the first of March. Scarcely any snow fell during this winter, and this led many to predict a drouth the next summer, which was not the case. The roads were of first class order all winter long, and two of our farmers, (R. Coughlen and J. M. Hagaman) improved the opportunity to haul their crop of corn to Fort Riley and Junction City. The price realized was two dollars fifty, and three dollars a bushel. Fifty and fifty-five bushels were hauled at a load. One hundred and fifty dollars for a wagon load of corn was not thought to be a bad price!

There was scarcely any buffalo hunting done this winter. The risk was not worth the sport and profit.

To show the kind and fraternal feeling the Government had for its frontier subjects, and the great wisdom that characterized its course, we must mention the fact that a scout, whose duty it was to ramble over the country and watch for and report "Indian signs" was employed at $125 a month and sent out here to the front. His name was George F. Oakley, and he was about as well fitted for that duty as Madam Bernhardt would be for a farmer's wife. Mr. O. was a graduate of the typo department of the Rochester Democrat and had never known hard work in his life, nor what it was to "rough it." He boarded on Elm Creek during the winter, never going once on a scout.

1865. There is but little to make history of this year. The rain-fall was not heavy, but it came timely and the corn crop was fair. Other crops were very good. There was not much disturbance from Indians and for this reason a large number of people came to the county and took claims. Buffalo hunters pursued their sport without much molestation.

The slaveholder's war closed in April, by the surrender of Gen. Lee, and the beneficent effects of peace were felt on this far away frontier.

The winter of 1865-6 was a severe one. Snow fell the middle of November, the fall weather prior to that time having been magnificent. Following the first flurry of snow the weather became intensely cold. Work on the Pacific Railroad, Eastern Division, which had progressed nearly to Manhattan, ceased, and was not generally resumed until Spring. A short period of sunshine and warm weather and then more snow, about eight inches followed. There were over three months of wintry weather.

The first political convention ever held in the county was held this year in October at the house of Moses Heller on Elk Creek. In it was represented, Shirley, Republic and the Republican Valley portion of Washington, and the object was to nominate a candidate for the legislature. The convention was held at the instance of the Rev. R. P. West, who wanted to go to the legislature. Out of mischief, more than anything else, the Shirley folks determined to contest for the candidacy, and they selected, as their victim, J. M. Hagaman. The convention was called to order and the voting begun, when the Rev. West found himself in the minority! In this dilema a happy thought struck him and that was to count those "whom he knew to be favorable to him." This was agreed to on the condition that the other side should be allowed the same privilege. Mr. West presented his proxies, which, it seems he had slyly provided himself with, and then Mr. Oakley, who was managing the case of Mr. Hagaman, presented his proxies, which to the astonishment of the Rev. West, considerably outnumbered his! Considerable quibbling and speech-making followed and the convention finally adjourned without making the nomination. Mr. West ran as an Independent candidate, but was badly beaten.

One day, in the month of October, a party of Wichita Indians camped just above the settlements on Elm creek, and busied themselves during the day begging of the settlers. The latter freely gave them, That night they stole 6 horses. Messengers were sent over the country and at sundown the next day a party of fourteen men, well armed, began the pursuit. Being mounted on good horses and the trail being easily seen in the bright moonlight, the thieves were overhauled as day began to dawn. Hobbled horses were first discovered, and a halt being ordered, Lewis Cassel and J. M. Hagaman were delegated to reconoitre the camp. This delicate work was so carefully performed that the position and numbers of the Indians were found. Returning without having caused the least alarm, they notified the party of the result of their reconoisance and a council was held to decide whether to kill or capture the enemy. It was decided not to kill unless they showed fight. J. M. Hagaman was chosen to lead the attack. He divided the men into three squads, with eight in the first line, four in the second, and two in the third. They were to march so that the squad of four was to come over a hill that intervened just as the eight aroused the sleeping savages. The object was to make the Indians believe that we had more warriors in reserve. The plan worked well. The first line rode up to the Indians before they knew of their presence, which was discovered by the chief's wife. She alarmed the rest and in less time than we can tell it they were on their feet and tightning their bows. It looked exceedingly war like at this moment, and the men appealed to their leader "for God's sake give orders to shoot." But the command was "not yet, keep cool." "There is an old Indian in the hollow with his rifle cocked and pointed at you," said one of the party, addressing the commander, but still he bade them hold their fire. During this exciting time the leader was parleying with the chief, all the time having his revolver cocked, and pointed directly at his heart with his finger on the trigger, so that had he been shot the chief would have been also. The naked body of the Indian was not more than two feet from the muzzle of the revolver. Perhaps it was the certain death of their chief that withheld the deadly bullet from our Captain.

Sternly and vehemently the old Chief denied any knowledge of the theft, and that his men had anything to do with it. To the truth of this he called God—the sun—pointing to it, to witness. As decidedly, and with equal emphasis our leader told him "You lie, you stole our horses last night and now have them." "When white man sleep?" said the old thief. "White man no sleep, saw you steal 'em."

He turned to his warriors and said something very much in earnest and they flung their weapons to the ground and jumped into the creek, swam over and rapidly disappeared in the timber.

A bloodless victory was won, and all that was left to do was to gather up the spoils and return. Thirteen ponies and horses and one mule, one superb target rifle, a number of blankets, some bows and arrows, powder-horns, moccasins and a few other articles were taken, all of which were agreed to be returned if they would return our horses in thirty days. They were never returned, and after making those whole who had lost, the remainder was divided among the fourteen.*

1866. This season was more favorable to the farmer than the two preceding it. All crops were good, but prices were low.

The influx of immigrants led the citizens to believe that they had enough to entitle them to an organization, and as their relationship with Washington County had become obnoxious to them they determined to cut loose from her. A petition was promptly signed and J. M. Hagaman delegated to present it to the Governor, which he did. The organization was effected on August 4th, by proclamation of Governor S. J. Crawford. Henry Lear, Moses Heller and George Wilcox were appointed Commissioners, and N. D. Hagaman, Clerk. Elk creek was made the temporary county seat. The election for county officers and member of the legislature was held on the general election day in November. The nominating convention was held the last week in August, and was held in the Elm creek school house. John B. Rupe was nominated for the legislature by the Republican party, and was

elected over J. M. Hagaman, Independent Republican.

The County officers elected were, Commissioners William English, Ed Neely, —————— Charles Davis, Clerk, Zachariah Swearngen, Treasurer, Quincy Honey Sheriff and——————.

In this first election the contest over the selection of the county seat began, and it was the chief issue in every election until it was finally settled in December 1869. The places voted for were Elk Creek (since Clyde) and Rochester. The latter place is two and a half miles east of Concordia, and was declared to be the choice of the voters, and so it remained until the election in 1839.

Elk Creek early became imbued with the idea that it was the center of the United States and that in time the brain and wealth of the nation would be located there, and around it, as the focal point, would revolve the whole universe. Its population was made up of sharpers, tricksters, scalawags, small fry politicians, with an occasional sprinkling of modesty and morality,— just enough of these elements to save it from brimstone and fire. They resolved to have the county seat located there, whether by fair means or foul. Every man, political or otherwise, had this object in view. All their efforts were bent in that direction. This, first, and then the capital of the United States!

There were men on the south side of the Republican river who were equally determined to have the county seat on their side, but while they lacked the cunning, the want of candor, the deceptive qualities that characterized their opponents, they were not destitute of shrewdness. They also had RIGHT on their side.

About the first work of Mr. Rupe, in the legislature, was to introduce a bill to divide the county in the center east and west, and attach the north half to Republic and the south half to Ottawa, and thus obliterate Shirley county. This action had been anticipated by J. M. Hagaman, and he had engaged the services of the member from Clay county to watch Mr. R., and report, which he faithfully did. Remonstrances against this ridiculously unwise act were circulated and were freely signed. They were put in the mail bag at Elk under the eye of a trusty friend and the bag watched until on its way east. When Mr. Rupe's bill came up on third reading the remonstrances were read and the bill lost its head on motion of a friend of the county to strike it off.

We have written of this matter at this late day because it is one of

---

* NAMES OF THE PARTY: J. M. Hagaman, G. D. Brooks, Lewis Cassel, G. F. Oakley, Richard Honey, James C. Neely, Quincy Honey, D. Heller, Caleb G. Thorp, Jacob Thorn, Charles Donoho, e. Cannot get the other names.—H

important county history, and not as a reflection upon Mr. Rupe, whom we highly respect. We have no doubt but what he is now as much pleased as we are that the scheme failed. We do not believe it was his idea. It was that of a different class of men, whom we have referred to as "sharpers and tricksters."

Mr. Rupe, like most new legislators, was bound to figure as an "active member," so he introduced another bill to change the name of the county from Shirley to Cloud. His reason for doing this, as we were informed at the time by a fellow member, was that the county was named Shirely after a "Trumpet" who used to figure around Fort Riley as a common prostitute. Mr. Rupe meant 'strumpet,' but an impediment in his speech made him make the mistake.

We do not believe the story of naming the county after Jane Shirley, the harlot. It is reported to have been done to tantalize Col. Phillips, who was the principal actor in defining the boundaries of this first tier of counties west and along the 6th principal meridian. As there were members in the legislature from Massachusetts, it is highly probable that it was named in honor of Governor Shirley of that State. It suits the writer better to have it so, at any rate, and that would not reflect upon the character and good sense of a Kansas legislature.

For the first time since the county was settled a delegate was sent to the Republican State Convention, and J. M. Hagaman had the honor to be the delegate. His expenses were paid by voluntary contributions made at the time, which we believe the first and only case of the kind that has ever occurred in the county. There was no Democratic party in the county then nor for several years thereafter.

This year the grasshopper pests first visited the county. They struck the county on the 30 of August, the day the Governor declared it organized, and which accidental occurrence was said by some of the blindly superstitious to be an unfavorable omen. The writer was on his return from Topeka and first rode into them three miles the other side of Clyde. The day was cloudless, yet the sun, which was two and a half hours above the western horizon, was totally obscured by the myriads of insects. The ground was speedily covered and trees bent under the enormous weight of the pests. In one case that came under the writer's observation a cottonwood tree six inches in diameter was snapped asunder. The moving pests almost blinded man and beast and spread consternation far and wide. Pen pictures cannot convey to the understanding of the enormous amount of grasshoppers that visited this county in 1866. A person who has witnessed one of those heavy snow storms that used to fall in the Adirondacks forty years ago, at which a foot of snow fell in a few hours, and then reflect that the grasshoppers were as thick as the snow flakes, he can form a tolerably good idea of the situation. We had not the re motest idea that there was a millionth part as many grasshoppers in the whole world; —where on earth did they all come from? They extended from Missouri over two hundred miles west.

The season was too far advanced and corn to hard to be injured to any great extent by them. The blades which were yet green, vanished, however, in the briefest space of time imaginable, as did every other green thing that suited their tastes, and they were not over fastidious in selecting. Red peppers and onions they relished and could make away with tobacco at a rapid rate.

Myriads of egg cones were deposited, each containing about thirty-five eggs. As the last half of the winter was mild millions of them hatched and died before maturing or reaching a conditon to do harm. In the spring there was much rain and the young were washed into the streams and swept away. Very little harm was realized from the new crop. Of course the old ones died, as they are annuals!

In May, this year, six men were massacred on Little Cheyenne, a tributary of Buffalo creek about six miles from Concordia. The party was composed of Lewis Cassel, Walter Haynes, William Collens, and Henry Collens,— Roberts——— Tallman. They were surprised on Brown's Creek, in Mitchell County, and after a running fight of fifteen or twenty miles the whole party was slaughtered on the head of the creek named. At first a fruitless search was made for them, but they were finally discovered by a second party and buried where they were killed. Subsequently their bones were removed to Clifton and re-intered.

This massacre did not cause a stampede of settlers, as had been the case in previous years. The murderous Indians were Cheyennes.

In July an outrage was committed upon the person of Mrs. John A. Morley on White Rock Creek. The Indians were Cheyennes.

Other outrages were committed, but they did not have the effect produced the preceding years. Immigrants continued to arrive daily and as the colonists grew stronger they became more confident.

1867. The snow fall was light this winter, at no time more than a few

12 HISTORY OF CLOUD COUNTY.

inches being on the ground at one time. February was warm and myriads of grasshoppers hatched and were destroyed by alternate freezing and thawing. March was warmer than February, and this with frequent rains, rid the country pretty well of the plague.

In April a massacre of settlers by the western Indians occurred. About the first of the month a party of Cheyennes came into the settlement, about twelve miles from the mouth of White Rock, and murdered three persons. Mrs. Sutzer, and her ten year old son and Nicholas Ward. A young man living with Ward, was shot in the neck while attempting to make his escape, was stunned but not fatally injured, and escaped and carried the news to the settlements. The person of Mrs. Sutzer was outraged after she was killed. There were nine Indians in the party and under the guize of being friendly Otoes were admitted into Ward's house. The dinner dishes were yet on the table and they asked for something to eat and were provided with it. Having finished their meals, one took down Ward's rifle, which lay in hooks attached to a beam overhead and shot him while he was unsuspectingly smoking his pipe. The two boys at this fled, but the Indians fired at them and brought both down. While they were out after the boys Mrs. Ward shut and barricaded the door, but the villains soon beat it down with an ax. Pillaging the house of what they wanted they made Mrs. Ward prisoner. Loaded the mules, belonging to Ward, two in number, with their plunder, started on their homeward march, making their fair prisoner trudge on foot.

Immediately on word being received by the settlers in Cloud and Clay counties two parties, without any knowledge of each others intentions, one from the north and the other from the south started to the scene of the murder. They arrived the same day, but the former in the morning and the latter near the close of the day. G. D. Brooks led the first party and J. M. Hagaman the party from the south side of the river. As the writer accompanied the last named party, and therefore knew what it did, will give an account of it.

The party left Elm Creek in the morning, all mounted and armed and rations for several days. The route chosen was up the south side of the river to Buffalo Creek and thence up that creek to a branch called Salt—sometimes Marsh—Creek which bore to the north-west. Shortly after passing beyond the head of it we came upon a flock of deer and "took one in." Reaching the slope of White Rock we discovered mule and Indian tracks. The trail was followed some distance, but

night approaching it was abandoned and the party hurried on and reached the scene of the murder as before related.

The opinion prevailed with the Elk Creek party that Mrs. Ward was either crazy and rambling somewhere on the creek or that she had been murdered. It was the Elm Creek party that solved the problem, led by J. M. Hagaman, and not by the Elk, or Brook's, party, as F. G. Adams has it in his "Homestead Guide," and as other writers have stated. Our party started the next day about noon and soon struck the trail. Two miles, or so, in a thicket of bushes the Indians had made a halt, and what else was done beside eating a meal can only be conjectured. Our party passed on, but with great difficulty kept the trail. The Indians had emptied the feathers out of the feather beds, leaving of course a few clinging to the ticks, which were shook and blown off as they traveled. This trifling thing enabled us to follow the trail where else it would have been impossible to follow it. A lady's drawers was found and the scabbord of a revolver. But on crossing streams the foot prints of a woman's foot was discovered and thus the mystery was solved. Mrs. Ward, undoubtedly, purposely stepped into soft ground so that her tracks might be seen by her would-be rescuers. We followed the trail to Limestone and there was forced to abandon the pursuit. It was useless, anyway to go further, as there were but twelve men in our company and the Indians had several days the start. Mrs. Ward has never been heard from. It is to be hoped that death kindly relieved her from a fate much worse. She was of frail build, aimable and fair looking.

The news of this massacre so alarmed the most exposed settlers that some of them withdrew to a place of greater safety, but after a while things settled down to their wonted quiet.

The summer was very wet, almost daily showers falling through the months of June and July. The crop yield was large and the prairies were covered with a very heavy growth of grass.

The county Republican Convention, this year met at the same place it met the year before, and nominated J. M. Hagaman for the legislature. The Elk creek people plied their customary deceptive arts and slyly brought out Jas. T. Donoho as their candidate. Mr. Donoho himself, was not given to divulging secrets and therefore did not let it be publicly known that he was a candidate until near the eve of election. The worthy! people of Elk poured into the ears of the friends of Mr. H. the strongest professions of friendship, and assured them that there was "no reason to fear as the candidacy of Donoho was only a joke and he would not get a half dozen votes." Of course the very innocent friends of Mr. H. believed their "tales of love!" Mr. H. was elected by a small majority.

The reader of to-day, who is a stranger to those early times, may wonder why the contests over those petty offices were so sharp and so strongly contested, but the reason is to be found in the fact that they all had "county seat" in them, and only one who has been through one of those internecine strifes can realize the earnestness, and bitterness, and the rascality, that are sometimes resorted to. The struggle in this county was incessant for seven or eight years, beginning when there were not one hundred settlers in the county. The north had the advantage of the south side of the river in that it had a good public road, built by the government, while the south side had no road at all. This was an important point in favor of Elk, as the river was hard to ford. Old Mr. Heller once tried to ford it on horse-back and the horse got stuck in the quick-sand and Mr. Heller came near loosing his life. He never tried it again. This story he told to hundreds of immigrants and very many were kept from coming to the south side, and some from settling in the county. The race was a race for voters and the "north" and the "south" kept about even for 9 years, and until the final election that decided the demoralizing contest.

As we have given Mr. J. B. Rupe the benefit of some of his work in the legislature we deem it but right to mention a part of the work of his immediate successor, and shall pursue this course with others.

The fifth bill introduced in this legislature was his bill to make a hedge fence a lawful fence as soon as planted. This met with bitter opposition from the farmers and cattle men in the House, and it would not have received a score of votes had a trial come. It was objected that it would almost prove the destruction of fences, and in that they were probably correct, unless "hedge" is a "fence." The bill was allowed to retain its place on the calendar, and a substitute was passed that was ruined by a southern Kansas cattle man. The bill left the matter of adopting the law with the Board of County Commissioners, but that selfish man, who looked solely to his own interest, would not leave it with boards of commissioners, and the people of the county, and asked to have his county, Coffey, excluded, and it was done. This made the bill special, instead of general and therefore unconstitutional, as a general law was

appliable to the whole state. It was so decreed to be by the Supreme Court.

The object contended for two years later became the settled law of the State.

Another measure was the amendment to the cost bills before Justices of the Peace in criminal cases. This made the prosecuting witness, if the person against whom he made complaint was not convicted, liable for costs.

The benefit to the tax-payers of this law has been very great. Prior to its passage one of the greatest burdens to the counties was the enormous cost bills in petty criminal cases before Justices. Shawnee county had $60,000 of such costs to pay the year before this law was passed. Cloud to-day would have $20,000 to pay annually but for this law. It was one of the most corrupt systems in existence. Constables and justices would connive together to trump up cases for the fees that were in them, just as U. S. deputy marshals and circuit court commissioners now do. A million dollars are stolen annually by those officers and the abuse is rapidly increasing.

A third measure was the introduction of a resolution to amend the constitution so as to allow all persons who are taxed for the support of the State Government to vote without regard to color, sex or nationality.

Strange to say no one could be got to champion this eminently just and important measure. Cowardly members admitted it to be founded on principles of right, but at the same time voted to kill it.

The general revision of the laws of Kansas was done by this legislature.

On the 25, of July occurred the brutal murder of a respected and industrious farmer and the dangerous wounding of another by two German Jew peddlers.

These men had a team of mules and wagon, and were peddling dry goods and notions. They came from Leavenworth, but whence to that place we do not know. At Elk creek, and other places, they inquired for two other peddlers, who preceded them with a covered wagon, and learned that they would soon return. Leaving Elk creek in the afternoon about sundown they crossed Upton creek, and drove to a place of security north of the road, and out of sight of anyone passing along the road. Here they remained for two or three days waiting and watching for their intended victims, and at length a covered wagon hove in sight. Hastening to the point already selected, they waited their opportunity. The road, at the crossing of Upton at that time, went into the creek at right angles with the stream and then turned suddenly to the right and out in a diagonal direction. The west side bank of the creek had been worn into a deep gulch by the wagon travel and this, with the sunflowers, weeds and grass on either side, hid the drivers from view from the place of concealment of the murderers on the opposite side until they reached the bed of the creek, or nearly there. As soon as enough of their bodies were exposed to their sight they fired, first at Bump and then at Davis, the first being hit in the neck, and expired almost instantly, and the other in the right lobe of the lung. The weapon used was a double-barreled shot gun loaded with bird shot, and the distance fired was about thirty feet. Bump was driving and as he fell dead Davis took the lines and drove down to Elk, where the foul act was made known, and spread rapidly over the country.

The next day a party of men pursued and captured the murderers at McBride's on Mill creek, in Washington county, and took them back to Elk, where they were examined before a justice of the peace on a charge of murder and held for trial at the next term of the District Court of Clay county. The following night they were taken from the custody of the sheriff and lynched. Thus ended the career of two black hearted scoundrels.

A more deliberately planned murder, and one more systematically carried out, never took place.

But they missed their mark. The intended victims escaped and two buffalo hunters received the deadly messengers meant for them. Strangely enough the men they intended to kill, the two peddlers, were met by them on their return trip, in less than an hour after they had killed Bump and wounded Davis. What terrible emotions must have thrilled them as they beheld the very men, in the full vigor of life, they supposed they had murdered! The names of the murderers were Richard Kennup and Edward Zacharias. A coroner's jury sat upon the bodies and its verdict was: "Come to their death by hanging by the hands of parties unknown to the jury." The verdict was supported by the evidence. Some of the jury and most of the witnesses were those who took part in the hanging. The evidence of guilt of the men was conclusive, but in addition to the evidence before the Justice their interpreter, Fred Chapauskie, overheard a conversation between them in which one accused the other of planning and getting him into the difficulty. Their bodies were buried between sections 30 and 29, range 1 west and about east of the north elbow of Elm creek.

The grasshoper pests visited the country again this year, coming the 27th day of August. They were not so numerous as they were the year before, but as they came earlier they did more damage. Again the earth was filled with eggs.

The winter of 1867-8 was warm and dry. Not more than four inches of snow was on the ground at one time. Some days the weather would be oppressively warm.

1868. Perhaps the spirits of the farmer was never higher; never was he more sanguine of good crops in prospect than were the farmers of Cloud county in the spring of 1868, and never were they worse disappointed. A very fine rain fell the 6th of March, and after one of the most dismally black days. Quiet in the atmospheric world succeeded the wind and rain storm. Grass sprang up and the whole country was, as if by magic, suddenly robed in green. The forests budded and leafed a month earlier than usual. Corn planting was well along in April. The mercury rose to one hundred as early as the middle of this month. Indeed July and August weather usurped the months of March and April. Light showers, followed by clear sky and a burning sun, came weekly and bi-weekly. Hot winds set in the 15th of June, and so fierce were they that it was difficult to breathe and face them. On plowed ground this was much worse. The last rain, for five weary weeks, fell June 28th. The eleventh of July corn was all tasseled and a better prospect for a first-class crop at this time of the year never occurred, and yet *not one field of ten or fifty acres yielded one bushel of corn!* Here and there on the lowest bottom lands was a little corn, but none whatever on the second bottom and higher land. To add to the misfortunes of drouth, on the 7th of August along came the grasshopper scourge and swept away what the drouth had spared.

Although corn was a failure, potatoes and other vegetables nearly so, on some favored places spring wheat was a fair crop. This was on ground broken the previous year and not planted. The sward had served as a mulch and prevented the evaporation of the water, which fell copiously in 1867, and being retained in the soil it nourished the plant of 1868.

Some assistance was received this year and the next until a crop was raised, by the settlers, from the more fortunate farmers in the eastern portion of the state.

On the 11th of July, Joseph Nicholas Hagaman, father of N. D., W. H. and J. M. Hagaman, was brutally murdered by William Harmon. Harmon was arrested and examined before Justice of the Peace Sears and committed to the Riley county jail to await his trial for murder in the first degree, but owing to the laxity of the criminal law and the venality of the sheriff of that county he escaped from the jail and was never again apprehended.

INDIAN RAIDS AND MASSACRES.

Of all the Indian raids on this border those of this year were marked with more cruelty, rapine and murder than all that preceded them, and for them the government of the United States was directly responsible. Of the intention of the savages to make the raid it was duly informed, yet it heeded not the appeals of the threatened frontiersmen. It had plenty of money and idle soldiers, could just as well as not have intercepted the raiders and saved the lives and property of the settlers. But every raid on the settlements by the savages is money in the pockets of Indian Agents and there is always a cord of sympathetic feeling between those agents and the government. It was generally understood that the election of a U. S. Senator cost the agent of the murderous Cheyennes and Arapahoes $50,000 and he must steal this amount to get even. If there ever was one that quit stealing when he was "even" we should be pleased to have his name. Nine tenths of the border troubles come through the weakness or villainy of the Indian agents. But why write of this? Everybody knows it. We want the people of future ages to know it, too, that is why we write of it.

Benjamin White, with his family, settled on Granny creek in 1866.* They were the most advanced settlers at that time in the valley of the Republican. He, like too many others, refused to believe that the raiding Indians were the wild ones of the West. In a conversation with him at our house on one occasion we were trying to impress upon him the certainty that it was the Cheyennes and Arapanoes, with possibly a small band of the Brule Sioux, that were doing the mischief, and so far succeeded as to get him to admit it possible. After thinking of the matter awhile he remarked: "If I believed as you do I would not leave my family there another day." But he would not "believe" and lost his life in consequence of it.

On the 15th, day of August 1868, Benjamin White and three of his boys were making hay on the river bottom north of buffalo creek, and about three miles from his house, and three mounted Indians rode up to them. Mr. White started to go to his tent and when walking in that direction one of the Indians shot him in the back and he fell to the ground. The boys run for the river and were pursued a short distance by the Indians; but not caught; who then gathered up White's horses and left. Neither Mr. White or his boys opposed them from the first to the last.

On the opposite side of the river, and

only a short distance from where this tragedy occurred, were N. H. Eaves, Wm. English and Charles J. English, his son, Robt. Atteberry and Virgil A. Brown at work in the hay field and in full view of the scene. The only weapon they had was a shot gun, taken along for the purpose of shooting wild turkeys and prairie chickens; not even suspecting an incursion from Indians.

Although but three Indians made their appearance, it is very likely that many more were in the hills out of sight, and ready to render assistance to the murderers, if they should be in need of it.

Mr. White was a hard working and frugal man and an exemplary citizen. Had ventured west to secure homes on the public lands for his family, which numbered six children. The beautiful valley of Granny creek so fascinated him that, though the danger of destruction daily beset him and his family, he could not make up his mind to quit the enchanted place and go to one of safety. But another sad part of his misfortune is to be told.

At the same time the Indians were murdering Mr. White another party was raiding his house, four miles away. Unsuspected they entered the dwelling and commenced their customary work of appropriating such things as they wanted. Alarmed, the family fled, but one girl, Miss Sarah, aged about 16 years, was caught and carried away into captivity. Six months afterwards Miss White was rescued by Gen. Custer in northern Texas. The rest of the family, including Mrs. White, escaped to the woods and were not discovered by the Indians.

The murder of Mr. White was the only one that occurred in the Republican valley this year, and Miss White was the only one carried away.

This party of marauding Indians was pursued 200 miles by Captain B. C. Sanders with 60 men, but they failed to come up with them, or to determine positively which direction they had gone, and the fruitless search was reluctantly given up and the party returned home.

CHAPTER IV.
THE SOLOMON MASSACRE.

The first settlers of Solomon Township were John Hillhouse, Robert Smith and James Hendershot. They settled in January 1866.* The same year, in April, H. H. Spalding and M. D. Teasley; in May John Higgins, ——Howard and Hewett; in July, Mc-

*Named after James Hemington, an eccentric old bachelor, who settled there in 1864. It has since been named White's creek, after Mr. Benjamin White.

*Mr. N. H. Eaves feels sure that Mr. H. C. Snyder, from whom I got this report, is incorrect as to the time of settlement, he thinks it was a year earlier. A H. Spalding says his brother H. H., settled in 1865, built his cabin and put up hay, but no other settlement was made that year.—H.

Minn, Mann and —— Wilcox; in November, H. C. Snyder, W. E. Mitchell Thos. Jones, Hiram Jones, E. J. Calhoun, W. T. Williams, and J. A. Potts. Sometime during the summer H. H. Dalrymple, I. N. Dalrymple and L. W. Jones settled.

In the spring of 1867 the settlement was thrown into intense excitement by the sudden appearance of 315 Pawnee Indians, but they proved themselves to be friendly by molesting no one and stealing all they could.

Later on in the season John Higgins was killed on Oak Creek in Mitchell Co. The place is now called Higgins Bluff. The Indians who did the deed were supposed to be Sioux.

The excitement over this murder had scarcely subsided when the great raid of August occurred.

Near the place where Glasco now is Miss Jeannie Paxton was teaching school, and report came of Indians in the neighborhood. She immediately sought safety for herself and pupils and started for the nearest house. Heroically placing herself between the fleeing children and their cruel pursuers, she reached the house in safety with all except Davis Snyder, who lingered behind to get something he thought essential. He was shot and left for dead, but recovered. During this raid Henry Hewett, Jonn Batchey, John Wear, and Benjamin Misell were killed, and Mrs. Henry Hewett, and the son of Hon. H. C. Snyder, Davis, were wounded.

Two months from the date of this raid another was made lower down the river and in addition to carrying away several head of horses the Indians captured and carried away Mrs. Morgan. She was recovered from them within a year afterwards by General Custer.

Peace reigned till spring when another raid was made, but this time without the loss of human life. The settlers had constructed a stockade and took the precaution to be near enough to it to get into it when the "red devils" were around. Several horses were stolen and successfully made off with.

With this ended the Indian troubles in the Solomon, and thereafter the country settled rapidly and they prospered in their chosen pursuit of agriture.

THE REPUBLICAN VALLEY.

About the first of October, 1868, a militia company was formed, B. C. Sanders was Captain and G. D. Brooks 1st. Lieutenant, and the services performed by this company, which were very considerable, gave protection as well as encouragement, to the settlers. In the Solomon Valley, in October of this year another company was formed with John A. Potts, Captain, and which performed considerable military service.

But this Valley was yet to be visited by another marauding band of Indians. Homer Adkins lived about six miles up the Republican from where Concordia is located. He had lived there since February 1868, and unmolested by the Indians.

June 2, 1869, Mrs. Adkins had occasion to send her son Ezra over the river to a Mr. Nelson's on an errand, and requested him to drive back the cows, which she thought she saw among the hills north of Mr. Nelson's. The boy did the errand and then went to the place where his mother saw, as she thought, the cows, and rode into a squad of thirty or forty wild Indians. He turned his horse instantly and rode for life toward home, the Indians following and shooting at him but without effect. He made the mistake a boy of his tender age, 12 years, was likely to make, dismounted and ran into the brush and among the sand hills, hoping, doubtless, that the Indians would take the horse and not pursue him. In this he was mistaken. Two Indians followed and shot him while the others secured the horse. His mangled body was recovered that night and brought to his grief stricken mother, almost in whose presence the foul murder was committed.

During this chase and work of death the family of Mr. Nelson fled and were saved, but their horses and their goods were carried off by the Indians.

Another raid earlier than this, at Scandia, and the Indian troubles were ended and peace reigned all along the frontier.

Scandinavians had settled that country Being warned of the danger of Indian depredations they took precautions against them, but, like many others abandoned them just as danger was near. They had withdrawn their sentinels from the hills and dreamed of security and happiness, just as a party of savages appeared in the neighborhood. Two boys were herding horses and the savage brutes rode down upon them, killing one, but the other luckily escaped. Five horses made up the booty, and the Indians made good their escape.

Thus ended the Indian troubles, which had lasted nine years, keeping the settlers in the most trying unrest, and subjecting them to heavy losses in time and means.

At the Republican convention, this year, I. N. Dalrymple, of Solomon township, received the nomination and election to the House. Mr. D. made a very active member, but we do not remember of any special measure he was the author of.

1869. The winter of 1868-9 was alternately cold and warm with but little

snow. The spring opened favorably
and a good crop year was predicted
which was fulfilled. Immigrants poured
into the country, and it now seemed
certain that the county was on a safe
and sure road to prosperity. The people flattered themselves that the Indian
troubles had ended, and that henceforth
they could dwell in the land they loved
so well in peace.

But again their hopes were to be
blasted and their dreams of peace and
happiness were again to take their customary flight to the realms of doubt and
uncertainty. As before related, a son
of Hanah and Homer Adkins was murdered by the Indians in sight of his
fathers house. A number of horses
were stolen, and several other less important depredations were committed
by the Plains Indians. There was a
sudden check of Immigration to the
front, but in a few weeks it was again
renewed and a continuous stream
flowed on for several years.

SETTLEMENT OF THE COUNTY SEAT DIS-
PUTE.

It had been very plain to the observ-
ers of county matters for some time
that a crises was approaching on the
county seat question. A good road had
been surveyed and opened on the south
side of the river from Junction City and
Fort Riley and over it daily was seen
the snowy covered wagon of the immi-
grant journeying on to the westward.
This route brought him over the best
portions of the Republican valley and
his eyes fell with longing desires upon
the beautiful bottoms of the river and
creeks, and the gently rolling uplands,
and, fascinated with the enchanting vis-
ion of a home and a competance in this
land of beauty and sunshine, he cast
anchor, and built his cabin or made his
"dugout" in the hill side.* Elm, Oak and
Wolf creeks, with their timber skirted
windings and rich alluvial soil, were soon
taken up and the homestead seekers
spread out on the magnificent table

* DUG-OUT - I do not know the origin of this
name. I never saw one and never hear of one
until I came to Kansas. For the benefit of my
readers a thousand years hence I will describe
the true "Kansas dug-out." It is a cellar dug
in the side of a hill, any size desired. Its height
can suit your taste and conve le ce, but is usually eight feet to the roof. The sides and inner
end are formed by the earth. Heavy timbers,
usually two go from end to end in the middle,
and then reaching to the sides poles are laid,
and on the poles straw or hay, some thin es brush
first nd then strnw, and on this a sufficient quantity of dirt is put to keep the rain
from penetrating through. A place for a door,
sometimes a door, but often a blanket I hung
up to keep the cold out, then a six-light win-
dow and you have it in true Kansas style. One
room answers for bed room, dining room and
kitchen However, they can be made much
better than this and many have been. I have
seen men worth several thousand dollars living
in "dugouts."

lands lying between the numerous
streams.

If the Republican valley offered superior advantages as to quantity the
Solomon valley was not inferior as to
quality, and the hitherto dim trail from
Abilene up the Solomon became, this
year, a hard beaten thoroughfare. The
lands along the river and creeks, rich
beyond all caulculation in the elements
that produce the golden sheaf and
shock were speedily taken, and yet the
demand was for ' more homesteads."

But while the "south" was actively settling up her territory the "north" was
not the less active. The land on that
side of the river was scarcely inferior to
the land on the south; but there was not
so much of it. About one seventh of
the county lies north of the river.

In the spring of 1869 that little fraction
had more voters than there was in
the rest of the county! At the first county seat election the south had just five
the most, but they were not all united
on Concordia.

In the spring of this year the "town of
Lake Sibley," which, prior to this had
only an embryonic existence in the brain
of Mr. A. A. Carnahan, began to im-
prove. Mr. C. M. Albuson, an agent of
the Scandinavian society, secured an
interest there and began to expend the
company's money in the erection of
buildings. Swenson, of Junction City,
was induced to take an interest, and
Albuson was supplied with goods and
farm implements by him. Lake Sibley
prsented quite a lively appearance this
year, which fact did not tend to make
happy the "millionaires"—in imagina-
tion—on the south side.

The autumn came, and with it the
customary convention from which bud
the future statesman. The usual struggle by the factions for the mastery, and
victory declared in favor of the south.
B. H. McEckron received the nomination for the lower house, but was defeated by A. J. Shelhamer, of Buffalo In
dependent, who intrigued with the
north side for its support.

A petition had already been in
circulation asking the County Board
Commissioners to order an election to
determine the relocation of the county
seat and was duly signed. This had
been moderately opposed by the leaders
of the south side in order to throw the
responsibility upon their opponants
and thereby make some capital against
them by charging them with precipitat-
ing the election to defeat what would
surely be the will of the people of the
county if it was more generally settled.
This had the desired effect. The friends
of a more central location of the county
seat than Clyde or Sibley were fully
aroused and worked energetically to
defeat the "north side schemers," who

sought their own interest and not that of the public!"

The laws of the U. S, set apart to all new counties a quarter section of land, which was to be laid off in town lots and sold to the best advantage and the money made out of the sale to be used in the erection of public buildings. Sometime in August parties filed on the south half of the south west quarter of section 33 and the north half of the north west quarter of section 4, T. 6 R. 3 west, in the name of the county for this purpose.

But up to the time of the convention the county seat, that was to be—had no name and the delegates to the convention from the south side of the Republican were requested to give it a name. Several were suggested and finally CONCORDIA was proposed by H. C. Snyder, of Solomon township, and in view of the harmony existing among the delegates, was unanimously adopted.

The Board of Commissioners met and ordered the election to take place on the 21st day of December. There were three contestants, Concordia, Clyde and Lake Sibley, and the result was Concordia and Sibley each, had more votes than Clyde which left the latter out in the cold.

The law of settling county seat locations then was that if no place voted for received a majority of the votes cast another election should be held two weeks thereafter and the voting confined to the two places receiving the highest number of votes at the first election.

Now the fight began in earnest. Never did contending armies battle with more zeal and energy than did these contending factions.

Sibley had the prestige of a real town, having a good store, a large hotel, and several dwelling houses, while Concordia had not a building, yea, not even a birds nest!

C. M. Albuson, A. A. Carnahan and L. B. Hay were the persons most interested in Sibley, and G. W. Andrews, William English and the writer had the deepest interest in Concordia. To those parties the stake was a big one. In the matter of dollars there was "thousands in it," and each determined to win if it took 'thousands' to win. The Sibleyites had an element to secure votes that the Concordians had not—whiskey—and they plied it freely. Mr. Albuson took a gentleman into a private room where there were a half dozen Scandinavians and several bottles, and Mr. A. personally informed him that "they was all right for Lake Sibley. Every one of them lived in Republic County. In less than two hours thereafter the writer was told it,—the man proved a spy in lieu of a friend" to Sibley. The next day Andrews was started out with or-

ders to "place more town lots where they would do the most good." The instructions were carried out satisfactorily and the plan worked charmingly!

During this contest there were two town companies interested in Concordia, J. M. Hagaman and G. W. Andrews and a silent partner forming one and W. McK. Burns, J. J. Burns Lee Burns, Isaac Burns, N. H. Billings and S. D. Houston Senior, the other. It is not to be supposed that they were idle pending the election!

Just prior to the first election Hagaman and Andrews surveyed and platted forty acres into a town site, adjoining the so-called county site, naming it 'Concordia,' and filed it in the office of the Register of Deeds.

The tickets being written,

For the permanent location of the county seat, Concordia; the north half S. W. quarter section thirty-three Town 5 and the north half of the N. W. quarter of section 4, Town 6 south of Range 3 west of the 6th Principal Meridian.

This was the only plat of Concordia, or any of the territory embraced in the limits of the city to-day that was on record in the Register's office at the time of the election, and hence was the county seat of Cloud County in connection with the tract named. Our object in making this statement will appear hereafter.

The election came and the liveliest one the county had ever known was witnessed. Every person of the male gender, who was old enough, and 18 was not too young in some cases, voted!

Concordia was victor! Clyde had proved false to her pledges to Sibley and gave Concordia eighteen votes. This vote turned the scale, by more than making good the loss Concordia had sustained by impracticable men who obstinately refused to vote for their own interest and that of the county.

The stranger to that contest who now looks over the county and has sufficient good judgment to discern the advantage of this location over that of Sibley will wonder that there should have been any opposition to Concordia as the Seat of Justice, yet had it not been for the great liberality of the town companies in the distribution of town lots Concordia would never have existed. Not one mile of railroad would there have been in this county south of the Republican river, except possibly, a few miles in the extreme north-west part of the county. Eighty per cent of the people would have been compelled to cross the Republican river every time they visited the county seat. Dissatisfaction over the location would have been great and frequent contests for re-location resulted. So that, no matter what means were resorted to to effect the location, the result has been a beneficent one. Scarcely a word of dissatisfaction over the choice has been heard from any source since the matter became settled, which was when the U. S. Land Office was located there.

CHAPTER V.

LOCATION OF THE U. S. LAND OFFCE.

1870. Although Concordia had received the popular vote for the county seat, the Commissioners elected at the November election refused to recognize it. The citizens in the vicinity of the embryo city erected a building for them to do business in and tendered it to the county free, and they refused to accept it. They held one meeting in it and before the next term they discovered it was not on the county tract and plead that as an excuse, and some of the builders were silly enough to move it onto that tract. For their pains, trouble and expense they met with the worst rebuff of all from the Board of Commissioners. They met at the April term and the roll being called and all present announced, a motion was made and carried, to adjourn to Clyde and they packed their duds and left, and the accommodating gentleman, who had put themselves to so much trouble and expense to overcome an objection that was not based on law or hog sense, were left to bite their lips and swear.

The evidence was too convincing not to be seen by the dullest person that Clyde and Sibley were again at work to thwart the will of the people in their choice of location of the seat of justice, and that stern measures must be resorted to to prevent its accomplishment.

About this time it began to be rumored that the Junction City Land District was to be divided and two new offices established, one at some point west on the Smoky Hill, and the other up the Republican.

The hope of securing the Republican Land Office revived the dying hopes of the friends of Lake Sibley and they at once began earnest work.

Sidney Clark, Representative from Kansas in Congress, whose time expired March 4, 1871, sought re-election, and, as a matter of course, he aimed to turn to the best advantage he could for himself, the location of these Land Offices, as well all federal appointments to be made in Kansas.

Mr. S. D. Houston, Sen., Receiver of Public moneys at the Junction City Land Office, was the "middle man" through whom Mr. Sidney Clark, and Senator S. C. Pomeroy, were reached by the Concordia Town Association, and G. W. Martin, of the same city, was the medium of communication of the Lake Sibley folks with Clark.

It was with the view of strengthening Clark in the county that B. H. McEckron was appointed U. S. deputy marshal, to take the census of Cloud County, which was made on the recommendation of members of the Town Company. When the County Republican Convention met to select a delegate to the Republican State Convention that should nominate or defeat Clark, J. M. Hagaman asked for and was made the delegate. This was a signal victory for Concordia, as her friends had not only the common enemy to contend against, but traitors in her own camp to beat and in this choice they were beaten.

Mr. A. A. Carnahan, the energetic and shrewd leader of the Sibley party, called a Mass Republican Convention and got himself elected a delegate to the same convention.

He was thrown out by the convention and Hagaman seated.

The combination against Clark was irresistible and he was floored. This misfortune threw a shadow over the prospects of the new town, but it had yet "a friend in court" in the person of S. C. Pomeroy, besides Clark had another session of Congress to serve.

Defeated for the House, Clark sought election to the Senate and now the race for a "Clark Representative" began in the county. Sibley put forward Joseph Berry, an early settler, but who lacked stability enough to acquire a homestead, even though he had the choice of the county. He was deficient in education, in ability and firmness ; without social standing ;—a very fair story teller—that was all. There was positively nothing to recommend Jo Berry for the position, yet he received the full vote of the north side of the river! Any other man would have done the same, as a show of success was all that was sought for by the enemies of Concordia. Had Mr. Berry been elected his vote for Sidney Clark would have been given on the condition that Mr. C. would secure to Sibley the Land Office, and on no other whatever. Pressed as Mr. Clark was by a pack of human vultures, ready to pounce onto him, it is unsafe to say what he would or what he would not have done under such trying circumstances.

When the new Board came into power, a majority of whom were chosen by the votes friendly to Clyde and Sibley, and in whose interest they were acting, at their first meeting, held Jan. 22, 1870, J. J. Burns, G. W. Andrews and J. M. Hagaman tendered an obligation, duly signed and secured, to erect a suitable building at the county seat for the county, if the Board would agree to have the offices removed there when it was ready for occupancy.

But with that same selfish spirit that characterized the conduct of the defeated towns from the inception of the contest years prior to this Mr. Dutton and Mr. Page indignantly rejected the generous proposition, the former remarking that he "opposed it because that would settle the location of the county seat at Concordia, which he did not think the people wanted."

The checkyness of this claim, will better appear, when the vote by which Concordia was made the county seat is considered; we see by the record above that in the first election Concordia lacked only _ votes of having a majority over both Clyde and Sibley and at the final election she had 46 majority out of a total vote of 29.

The simple truth is that Mr. Dutton, Mr. Page and their confederates, were striving their best to defeat the will of the people. And they continued to work at that until legal proceedings were about to be begun to compel them to do their duty, and then they sneaked to the county seat like whipped spaniels.

Mr. McEckron was elected by 81 majority, he receiving 238 to 157 for Mr. Berry.

So this scheme, concocted to defeat the will of the people in selecting the county seat, was thwarted and the 'schemers' brought to grief.

There were four buildings on the town site, now containing over a section of land, October first, 1870. One was owned by J. M. Hagaman, one by G. W. Andrews, one by A. A. Carnahan, the other was the county building, erected by the town company with the help of some of the citizens.

About this time work was begun on the Land Office building, and others immediately began to spring up. From this date the success of the town was assured.

The excessive drouth, this year, ruined the early corn crop, and seriously shortened the wheat crop. During June and July there was not rain enough to wet the ground half an inch. Wheat averaged about eight bushels to the acre, while early corn yielded nothing. This year was extremely favorable to lazy farmers, who through shiftlessness delayed corn planting till June. This came up and struggled along till the August rains and much of it turned out a fair crop. "Sod corn" also did well. This being planted in June received the benefit of the late rains and in some cases yielded twenty bushels to the acre. Frost held off till late in October.

United States Senators E. G. Ross and S. C. Pomeroy visited this county this summer, the latter going as far west as Cawker City. They were very much impressed with the country, its configuration, its numerous streams and the remarkable fertility of the soil. It was the good opinion of the county these gentlemen had which they took occasion to have largely circulated, especially the the latter, that influenced much of the large immigration of the next spring.

The United States census, taken this year for the first time, showed 2,323 population for the county. It was taken in June but before the close of December another thousand had been added.

1871. The winter of 1870-71 was very favorable for out door work, and as such it was very fortunate for the new town, as much business was planned and carried through.

It was equally as fortunate for the homesteaders, hundreds of whom took claims and made their dug outs or erected cabbins. In the spring the busy hum of industry was heard on every hand and the transformation of the wild prairie into farms went vigorously on.

This year the strong desire for a railroad took shape in the submission of two propositions to vote bonds, one to the Kansas Central and one to the Central Branch railroad Companies. The latter carried and the other was defeated. Neither was built.

In 1872 the Junction City and Fort Kearney Co., asked the County Commissioners to submit a proposition, but they refused, because the Company did not positively agree to come through Clyde.

Fire, this year, swept away a large portion of Concordia. The fire started in the building on the south east corner of 6th and Washington streets and burnt over nine lots. It occurred the night before Christmas.

1873. We pass this year without detaining the reader with the narration of unimportant events. Crops were short, the rainfall being stinted. The winter was mild and dry, very little snow falling.

1874. The most notable events of this were drouth and grasshoppers, both of which we had a surfeit. Protracted drouths threatened the destruction of corn and some other crops, and seriously cut short the wheat crop. Fortunately grasshoppers, in their old familiar style and quantities, put in an appearance.

They were intensely numerous and hungry, and destroyed what was green, in a very short time. A controversy, has been going on ever since as to whether the drouth or the grasshoppers destroyed the crop, but we see no reason for controversy, for if the grasshoppers had not come there would not have been a crop, and on the other hand, if the crop had been ever so good, the grasshoppers would have taken it

1875. This year the rains were timely and abundant, and a good crop was raised.

1876. Up to this date not a foot of railroad had been built in the county, and the people became very anxious to have a road. At length the "slow coach" of the Central Branch concluded to move, and its agent was sent here to ask the county for bonds. They were voted and on the 8th day of January 1877, the first locomotive whistle sounded in Concordia. The next year the road was built on to Beloit and Kirwin, and a branch to Scandia and Talmage, in Republic county.

The Junction City and Fort Kearney Co. asked for bonds to build to Concordia at the same time the Central Branch did, and was refused.

The first month of the operation of the Central Branch it took from Concordia 1,100 car loads of freight. The statement of the President, R. M. Pomeroy, is our authority for this. This remarkable trafic shows at once the great demand for a railroad in this county. We are satisfied that the extra price realized by the farmers on this and the next year's crop more than rendered an equivalent to them and the business men for the bonds given the road, $70,000.

The winter of 1876-7 was very mild and open. In January frequent light rains fell and kept the roads in a muddy condition. This year proved a very fair crop year, an average yield of the cereals were produced.

1878. This year passed without any noteworthy events and 1879 was ushered in with promising weather.

Growing weary of the Central Branch monopoly, the people of the county seat moved to procure another road and succeeded in getting an extention from Clyde of the Junction City and Fort Kearney. Their hopes of competition, however, were to be disappointed for ere the first train arrived the Central Branch had passed into the Gould system" and both went under his management.

1880-81-82-83 84, do not furnish topics of interest of a nature to warrant us in writing at length. Farming and business have constantly increased and flourished in a most satisfactory manner. This year, in the month of September, the fourth railroad was built into the county and the third one to the county seat.

The following map show the streams that water the county and the location of the principal towns.

Many important events have been omitted from the general history to be inserted in the separate history of the most important trade centers.

CLYDE.

Our separate history begins with Elk Township. The town and township were named after Elk Creek, which rises in Washington and Republic counties, flows southerly and empties into the Republican river one mile east of Clyde. The soil of this township is unsurpassed for richness. The surface along the river and creeks is generally level and away from them it is moderately rolling.

Elk township was settled in 1859. Mr. Parks and wife and several children, being the first settlers. Their claim was the "Old Heller place," as it used to be known, and comprised the territory, in part, where the Kansas Pacific depo stands. Mr. Park's claim shanty stood near the foot of the hill north of the Pomeroy House and was built of puncheon set up tight, and covered with dirt. In September or October Moses Heller and his two sons, David and Israel came. The last named were the first permanent settlers of Elk township. When the writer came to Elk, (July 8, 1860) Parks and his family had been subsisting on jirked buffalo meet for six weeks, and was very anxious to sell and get away. At this same date there lived in a house on the rise of ground west of Elk creek, — a log house erected by the Eaton Town Company,—Mr. Kearney, and his reputed wife and child. They were not married. This woman presented the most abject and poverty stricken appearance. She had but one garment on and that was so rent in many places that she had to hold the rents together to hide her naked body.

The condition of these two families was enough to discourage many people from seeking a home in the country, but this party soon discovered that the country was not responsible for their condition.

The last named claimed no settlement and left next month.

Charles and Peter Conkling and Jacob Heller, son of Moses Heller, were the next settlers. They occupied the house, just described, with the wife of Jacob Heller, who was a sister of the Conkling's. They also had another sister. Jacob Heller accidently shot himself shortly after he came there by pulling his rifle, muzzle to,remost, toward him from a wagon. The hammer caught on a bolt of shingle timber, with which the wagon was loaded, and slipped before it got to the half cock catch in the tumbler of the lock.

Mr. Heller was buried at Elk and was the first person buried there.

Emanuel Cline and wife came in 1861;

but made no settlement. They lived awhile with Moses Heller.

The early part of the summer of 1862, the postal route to Irving was extended to Clifton, and James Fox appointed postmaster, and in the autumn of that year it was extended to Elk and Moses Heller appointed postmaster. He held the office over fifteen years.

Mr. Heller's house was the general stopping place for travelers. He welcomed all who came and rarely took pay for entertaining them. He was a genial man social and generous to a fault. Moses Heller never went on a hunt for Indians, and his advice was rarely sought for. He staid right at home and minded his own business, and so did his son Israel. The latter never went on an Indian scout either and refused to let their horses go even under the most pressing demands for them.

This much is due to truth. We dont intend to allow the men who did the hard and dangerous work of protecting this border to be robbed of the credit due them for their great sacrifice, and given to those who did nothing. Elk township did less towards protecting the border than did any other settled portion of the county. If it furnished a single man to go on a scout the first four years of its settlement, we fail to recall his name.

In the spring of 1866 Cowls & Davis started a store in one part of Heller's log house, one load of goods comprised the stock, and the sales were rapid and the collections slow. A considerable portion of them are yet uncollected:

Mr. Charles Davis continued in business after the partnership of Cowls & Davis was dissolved and became one of the most prominent men of the town.

In the autumn of this year Andrew W. Smith, a worthy resident of Elk, conceiving the idea of raising some money by trapping on the Solomon, set out with his son Uriah and James Neely with this object in view. They fell in with a party of Otoe Indians and the mistake of Mr. Smith was that he did not remain with them. Neely and Uriah returned home with a load of buffalo meat and Mr. Smith remained. He was never again seen alive—nor dead—by his friends.

The story of the Indians was, made to the writer by the Chief, Big Soldier, that Smith remained a day or so with them and then went higher up the river, and that was the last they saw of him. We believe them. Hovering around in front of the Otoes, doubtless, were scouts or pickets from the wild tribes of the Plains, and into these Mr. Smith unknowingly went and was killed.

In the autumn of 1866 the Clyde Town Co., was "organized and Elk changed to Clyde. The growth of the town was

slow until 1869, when immigration began to flow into the county, since which time it has had a healthy growth. It has two railroads, an excellent school edifice, several churches some elegant dwellings, a large number of business houses, grist mill, two newspapers, the *Herald*, owned by John B. Rupe, and the *Mail*, owned by J. C. Cline. It has the honor, also of having the first newspaper published in the county, the *Republican Valley Empire*, started by Henry Buckingham,—since removed to Concordia. The population numbers about 1,500. She is one of the most enterprising towns of the west. Location, four miles south, and one and a half west from the north and east lines of the county and a half mile north of the Republican river.

It furnished two soldiers for the Union army, David Heller and Emanuel Cline.

We are unable to find any record evidence showing when Clyde was organized a city of the third class. But think it was in August 1871, as the Judgment of the Supreme court affirming the Judgment of the District court annulling the first organization was filed in the Clerk of the Court's office at this time.

SHIRLEY.

The first permanent settlement established in the county was on Elm Creek in July 1860. We have already referred to the persons who made it.

In the month of August, this year, these three families were the only persons residing in the county. Those who had previously made settlement left during the Indian excitement in July and none ever resumed their settlement. In 1861 William Chapanskie, and family, Fred Chapanskie and family, Mr. Weber, George Wilson. In 1862 Zachriah Swearingen and family, Richard Coughlen and family, David Robertson and family and Joseph Berry and family. From this settlement there enlisted in the Union army, Joseph Berry, Fred Chapanskie, George Wilson, Jacob and Caleb Thorp (sons of John M. Thorp) and David Robertson.

Elm, Beaver and Dry creeks run through the township while the Republican flows along the north and a portion of the east side. This was the third best timbered township in the county.

The town of Ames, in this township, is located on the right bank of the Republican and at the confluence of Elm with that river, and on the Central Branch. It has a depo, hotel, the largest grain elevator in the county, several stores, post office, livery stables, etc. The inhabitants number about 150. This town has a very pleasant location.

Many interesting incidents to frontier

life occurred in the early days among the settlers of this township, some of which it may be well enough to narrate.

Shortly after our settlement in July, the children came screaming into the house, (which stood on the bank of Elm creek where the wagon road now crosses it,) terror stricken and shouting "the devil, the devil just come right up out of the creek." Indians, was the first thought of the writer, and he grasped his rifle and carefully explored the place where his satanic majesty was represented to be by the half frightened to death children, and there he beheld, in all his majesty, a noble specimen of the bull buffalo. A shot from his trusty rifle and he fell dead in his tracks, and about twenty feet from the house.

Shortly after this, one night about 10 o'clock, Fenskie, who lived a quarter of a mile east, shouted, "Indians, Indians, Indians, come quick." We went "quick" not stopping to dress, but when we reached Fenskie's, the 'Indians' were gone;— they were wolves, after his soap grease!

One day in October '64 the writer saw a buffalo feeding near where Ames now is, and he at once determined to have him. The first shot from his rifle wounded him and he would have made his escape but for his dog who came at the crack of the rifle and engaged him in battle. Few dogs would tackle a buffalo, but this one would throat even an Indian if told to. Another ineffective shot and the bull became terrible. With his head near the ground and tail erect, he would again and again dash at the dog and fairly make the ground tremble with his bellowing. No events in the arena of bull fights ever surpassed this in the awful rage of the tormented beast. The bravery of the dog equalled the fury of the bull and with the most provoking indifference to his own safety he would play about the head of the infuriated beast, occasionally nipping his nose, or his heels if he turned to run. At length the bull yielded the contest and beat a retreat, but unfortunately the hunter was directly in the line of retreat and as, when maddened to frenzy, they never turn aside for man, his situation became perilous in the extreme. Half of the distance between them had been passed and the bull was now within fifteen feet of him, and his eyes, verily, flashing fire. To jump one side and let him pass seemed the only alternative, and instantly attempting this, he sprang, when, horror, the only button that held his buckskin pants flew off and down around his feet the cumbersome garment fell and he was anchored to the spot! At this juncture he yelled to his faithful dog "take him Jack," and he instantly seized the flying bull by the nose, was flung ten feet in the air and

entirely over him, the tremendious effort of the bull to relieve himself from the dog swayed him to one side and he passed the hunter within reach his of hand.

The interest of the reader has possibly created a desire to know what became of this buffalo. Gathering up his pants he followed him, with his limping dog, towards the mouth of Elm creek, whither he had fled, and making a button out of a piece of bush, he secured his pants against another like mishap! The bull went down the river bank and followed down the stream to the "Big Island" where he was again aroused and fled, but was brought to bay again by the dog, and shot about half a mile south of the lower end of the Island, just as dusk had so dimmed the sights of his rifle that he was obliged to take aim alongside of the barrel.

This was the farthest east a buffalo was killed in the Republican valley since its settlement in 1860.

One more and we shall have to close. One of the greatest pests to the frontiersman was the begging Indians. These were very numerous and troublesome. Dire vengeance was often threatened, but never carried into effect. One day in December, 1864, one came to the house of the writer and began his customary begging, much to the annoyance of his wife. The scout, G. F. Oakley, was stopping there, and having observed him for a while, he said, "Mrs. H. do you want this duck around here?" He was promptly answered in the negative, when he ordered him to leave. Blustering up he gave Mr. O. to understand that he would "go when he got ready," at which Oakley took hold of him, shoved him towards the door, and kicked him through it. Making haste to his pony he mounted, and when astride of him he shook his fist at Oakley, in a threatening manner. At this Mr. O. jirked out his revolver and fired at him, bearly missing him, and he flung himself on the opposite side of his poney and rode away as fast as he could ride. Reaching a neighbors house, where he had been given a squash, he hurriedly shouted, "give me squash, quick, God damn" he shoot Indian."

Of course "God damn" did not mean the writer as he was forty miles away?

LINCOLN.

This township is composed of ¼ of congressional township 6, and a portion of 5 range three west. It is bounded on the north by the Rpublican, nearly or quite fifteen miles of that river runing along its northern boundary. Portions of Oak and Wolf creeks pass through it and Lost creek takes its rise in it.

We believe that the credit of being the first settler must be given to a Mr. Wolf, who made his claim in 1859, laid the foundation for his cabin, which he completed the nextspring and moved into it with his family. He broke and planted and lived there until near the close of the year when he found it necessary to go to the settlements to get supplies to live on. He did not return, but afterwards some of his family did. (We are in doubt as to whether his claim was in Lincoln or Buffalo, but feel quite well assured that it was in the former)

To N. H. Eaves and family, however, is due the credit of being the first permanent settlers. They settled on the river one and a half miles north of Concordia November 2, 1865 and maintained their settlement. About the same time Richard Worst settled at the mouth of Lost creek. William English with his family in the spring of 1866. One part of his place adjoins the townsite of Concordia on the north. Joseph Decker settled on Oak creek, on the farm, now owned by Richard Coughlen, in 1867. Albert Green settled in 1867, his place joined the town of Concordia on the West. William Collins and family, settled in the spring of 1866. George Hibner and family settled in 1867. Wiliam Townsdin and family in the spring of 1867.

We believe the above to be all who located prior to 1868.

This last named year a few more settlers were added, among them G. W. Andrews and J. M Hagaman and family. At the election in November seven votes were polled.

As identified with the location of the county seat and the founding of Concordia, it may be well to give the reason for the writer leaving his home on Elm creek and taking a prairie claim in Lincoln. In August 1868, he had fully determined to settle in Clyde and build a hotel and follow the business of keeping it. To this end he sought the town company and asked it for a location. At first the members seemed quite anxious to have him come there and offered him an acre for a nominal sum. Two or three days later, and when ready to commence putting material on the ground, he called on Charles Davis to be shown the location and, to his surprise, he took him several lots further west and would give him but two lots for the money. The 'acre' could not be had at all. A change had evidently come over the minds of the Company. They did not want him there and he solemnly swore he never would settle there and that the county seat should "go west" and to Lincoln township, where it now is. Saying to Mr. Davis, "I'll see you again,' he bid him 'good day,' and the next day took up the claim that forms the town site north of the Central Branch road.

"County seat" and to "beat Clyde"

was his constant thought by day and his dreams by night, and this should be done if it took every ox, cow and horse he had.

G. W. Andrews happening along was induced to settle upon the mile strip along side of Hagaman's, under the assurance that it had "County seat in it," but that intention must be kept a "profound secret." Andrews was a "lucky catch," for he is the best worker up of any scheme we ever met. Strangely enough there were men, whose votes were essential in this contest, who would not "vote the County seat here if Hagaman wanted it here," and others, as silly, if Andrews was to be benefitted, or English, or Eaves, by it. Their votes were all secured, however, and the cost was not great!

Having dwelt upon the subject of this election in the general history, we shall not repeat it here, but confine our remarks to the

PROGRESSIVE HISTORY OF CONCORDIA.

Elevation Above Tide Water at the Point Where the Central Branch Road Crosses Broadway, 1,389 feet. Above Low Water in the Missouri at Atchison, 593.

The following clipped from the *Settlers Adviser*, published February 1872, by L. J. Crans & Co., is a fair description of Concordia at the time it was written:

"We can name with pride our county seat. Scarcely a year has passed since its organization and we now have a town in which all branches of business have several representatives. Concordia is beautifully situated on the right bank of the Republican river at a point which will allow an indefinite extension along the level bottom land. The southwestern portion is undulating and high, affording magnificent building sites—giving a fine view of the surrounding country and of the river fringed with timber."

The town site proper contains 515 acres and to this has been added about 100 acres more.

The business streets are 100 and 120 feet wide and the residence portion 80 feet wide. The alleys are 20 feet wide. The business lots are 22x132 feet and the residence lots 44x132. Around the outskirts the lots vary in size.

About 300 lots were given away by the town Co., to get the town under way, and for some time lots were sold at mere nominal prices to those who would build.

The diversity of lots from low and level to high and rolling, suit the peculiar and varying tastes of people.

The city is easily drained, thereby a healthy condition at moderate cost.

Water is easily obtained, and of the best quality. About 35 feet on the low ground, and 70 on the high ground secures a never failing well. Contamination from privy vaults is impossible, unless they are sunk to an unwarranted depth, which can be guarded against by ordinance.

Railroads have been mentioned in the general history.

The country surrounding the city and tributary to it presents as fine a landscape view as many of the most noted places of the world. It is an enchanting sight, in May, when the dreary brown of winter has been transformed to the cheery green of summer, to follow the winding of the timber skirted Republican and the lines of timber that indicate the numerous creeks; to feast the eyes upon the various slopes and levels, all covered with the vendure of spring.

But the *real* wealth is found *in* the soil. It is from this to a great extent, the millions must come to build up and enrich the town. To be sure manufactories will do their part, but they hold a secondary place in the process of building up.

The soil is here and all it needs is the hand of industry to make it produce the 'millions.'

Cheap fuel is of the highest advantage to a town, and this exists, and the supply is inexhaustible. Coal is being mined a mile south of the city.

The Republican river has been securely dammed and furnishes water power enough to run an immense amount of machinery. There is across the river the finest and best built dam in the state of Kansas, and no state can produce a better.

One of the finest, if not the most elegant and best school building in the State has just been completed. In school advantages the city will make it an object for people to send their children here from abroad to have their education finished.

In conclusion let us say, Concordia has had a steady, and therefore healthy growth, from the day she began her existance, and has, from all appearance, as bright a future in prospect as she has had in the past, and that is good enough. In point of intelligence and morals her 3,500 people are not behind the most favored in other lands.

When we consider the eminent progress Concordia has made in the few years she has existed, and the boundless resources of the soil and country around her; of her numerous capabilities for growth and expansion, may we not reasonably predict for her in the near future a city of 30,000 people. We so predict.

SIBLEY—LOCATION AND HISTORY.

The township of Sibley comprises

the territory on the north side of the Republican river and west of range two Two thirds of the township is river bottom, a small portion of the other third is moderately rolling and the remainder hilly. The productive qualities of the bottom land is equal to any other in the county and the same is true of the upland, compared with the same class of lands in the county.

In the north east part of the town are the coal mines, a very valuable industry.

Minersville is a village of some 150 inhabitants and located on the north line of the township. Has a store, post office, school house and public hall.

SETTLEMENT OF SIBLEY TOWNSHIP.

The first settlement of the township was made in the spring of 1860 by Sut McQuarty and John Allen. Both had families. Their places were about one mile north of the Lake. They built a double log house for accommodation of their families, broke eight or ten acres of prairie and planted it. They possessed cattle, horses, hogs, and chickens, and were very well fixed for new settlers.

One morning about the middle of July 1860, they were aroused by commotion among their fowls, and on looking out, to their utter astonishment, they saw Indians spearing their chickens Others of the dusky tribe were closely observing them through the cracks of their log houses. There was considerable commotion within that, heretofore, quiet domicile. There was "getting up and dusting," as one of the family told us. Indians were everywhere, "thousands of them," as reported at the time, and fear for their lives seized the whole household, and as speedily as was possible they put what they could of their furniture in their wagons, hitched on their teams and headed them eastward. Arriving at Elk creek they already found the settlers gathered there and prepared for war. Some hunters came in and reported three nations of warriors in the vicinity of Lake Sibley, the Cheyennes, Arapahoes, and Sioux together numbering 15,000. The situation was not a pleasant nor desirable one. The Indians were insolent, acting as tho they would kill at the slightest provocation. They were not given it, which is, probably, the only reason no one was killed.

The excitement at Elk was intense. Wives appealed to their husbands to leave the country and go to a place of safety. Five families intending to settle on Elm creek came one day and left the next, taking with them John Sheets and family, the Elm creek settler. Allen and McQuarty removed their stock as soon as they thought it safe and left for more congenial climes.

About the fifth day of the excitement

700 Pottawatomie Indians went west on a hunt and the wild Indians sought safety in retreat and the excitement was at an end.

Allen and McQuarty never again resumed their settlement.

Several families wintered at the Lake the next winter, but none became settlers at that time.

The next settler was A. B. Cross, who established his home there in 1862, and maintained it, with an occasional intermission.

Dennis Taylor and Dempsey, his son, established their residence in 1864. Bailey, and family, Michael Swartz and and Cornelius Reed came in 1866, and B. C. Sanders in 1867.

THE LAKE AND ITS NAMESAKE TOWN.

Lake Sibley is nothing more nor less than an old bed of the Republican, made by the river describing a large circle in the form of a horse shoe and then cutting a channel across the narrow end. The river drift closed both ends and left the pool that is known as the Lake. It is now a mile and a half long, but when formed must have been five or six miles. There was in the early days many fish in it, but they have been caught out faster than they bred.

Mr. A. A. Carnahan, of Concordia, located a quarter section of land a half mile north of the Lake in 1867, and dreamed of a city and worlds of wealth! Of course he had "county seat" in view, and to this end he labored with zeal and skill. In 1869 he had a portion of his land surveyed and platted it in a town site.

We have before spoken of the success and ruin of this town and the causes that lead to it and it is unnecessary to repeat them. A shell of a building remains where ten thousand dollars was once invested in buildings. The school house is yet in tolerable condition.

Sibley was the best timbered of any township in the county. In 1860 heavy timber existed between the Lake and the river with an occasional stretch of prairie, and extended westward and eastward along the river. On the west along the river, was heavy belts of timber.

LAWRENCEBURG.

The north part of this township lies between Elk on the east and Sibley on the west, and the south part between Shirley on the east and Lincoln on the west. The Republican runs through the middle of it. Frank Lawrence and his mother were the first settlers. The date of their settlement we are unable to fix, but think it was in 1863 or 1864. Nathaniel Fox, D. B. Hines, were the next settlers. All these settled on the north side of the river.

Salt creek rises in Republic county, runs south through the north part of the township.

The town of Lawrenceburg is located on Salt creek. The Kansas Pacific road passes through it and a branch of the same road runs to Belleville, the county seat of Republic county. The B. & M. road cuts the north-west corner.

The town has a depo, post office, store and grain elevator.

The settlement of South Lawrence is too modern to merit attention. The Central Branch runs through it near the south line. Lawrence was the second best timbered township in the county.

The town of Rice, in this township, is located on the C. B. road, has a store, post office and elevator.

STARR.

This township is located in the southeast corner of the county, and is congressional township 8, range 1 west.

We have no record of the first settler. Chapman creek rises in this township and flows south easterly and discharges in the Smoky Hill. There is not much level land in the township, but the soil is good. Here, in the autumn of 1860, the writer hunted buffalo, there being hundreds of thousands of them there.

Miltonvale, is located four miles west of the east line of the township and at the terminus of the Kansas Central. It is a city of the third class, with a population of five or six hundred. It has a good grist mill several business houses and a good hotel.

It has one news paper, the *Miltonvale News*.

GRANT.

Is the north-west township in the county, and one of the best. Buffalo creek runs through it from west to east and Cheyenne, a tributary, comes into it from the south.

Fourfifths of the land is creek bottom, and of the richest quality. Jamestown is located near the center east and west, but near the southern boundary.

This is an enterprising city of the third class. The Central Branch passes through it and the Mankato and Burr Oak branch starts out. The city contains about seven hundred people.

It was not far from this site of this town where the Western and the Eastern Indians had a three days battle in 1860, in which, we regret to say, not an Indian was killed.

Jamestown has a news paper, *The Kansan*, owned by Mr. Burton.

NELSON.

This township is composed of congressional township six, range two west.

George Greathouse and family were the first settlers. "Twin mounds," are on the west branch of Elm creek in this township and one of them is on the farm of W. B. Brisbine. On the summit of this high mound, in July 1860, were flourishing wild black currants. From its sides flowed no springs, not even was there an indication of one. Yet, since the settlement of that country a line spring sprung from the west side of the mound and not far from the summit.

There is a post office in Nelson township.

SOLOMON.

So much has been said of this township in the general history that not much more is left to be said. It is the south-west corner township, with the Solomon river running through it from west to east. The soil is fertile and well adapted to the raising of all the cereals and roots of Kansas.

The town of Solomon numbers about 200 people, has a good grist mill and newspaper, *The Sun*, Ferd Prince, proprietor.

SUMMIT.

So called because it lies on the hight of land between the Republican and Solomon rivers. It is a very good township of land. Has no village.

LYON.

Lies east of Solomon and west of Meredith. Is an excellent township of land. Too much uncertainty as to the first settlers to attempt to give them. Cool, is the name of the post office.

COLFAX.

Lies between Starr and Shirley with Aurora on the west, and in it Mulberry, the east branch of Elm Creek, Beaver and Dry creeks, take rise. It is wholly upland, but the soil is good. We have no record of the first settler.

AURORA

Lies west of Colfax and is congressional township 7, range 2 west. It lies nearly between the east and west branches of Elm creek. It is a good township of land. Do not know the first settler.

ARION

Wm. M. Wilcox and family are the first settlers of this township. It is among the best in the county. Has a post office and store.

MEREDITH

A Mr. Stone took a claim on Pipe creek in 1861, built his cabin and established his residence. In 1866 four families lived in the township, and quite a number of claims had been taken. Has a post office and store. This is congressional township 8, range 3 west.

OAKLAND

This township had claimants of land as early as 1861, but we cannot recall their names, nor can we determine whether they ever became settlers.

A portion of this township is rugged, but the soil is fertile. This is congressional township 8, range two west.

BUFFALO.

James Heffington was the first settler of this township, but abandoned his claim. Benjamin White was the first permanent settler.

We have said all that needs to be said of him and this township in the body of this history.

THE MILL ENTERPRISE.

In the month of November 1870 Hilliare Lanoue selected a site for a saw and grist mill, where it now stands, and in the month of December brought from Nebraska his engine, boiler and machinery and soon had the saw mill at work. A year or two afterwards he erected a stone building and put in two burrs and began to grind. In 1872 he commenced work on a dam across the Republican. This was an enterprise that few men, even with an abundance of capital to back them, would dare to undertake, but Mr. Lanoue, without any capital, plunged in and succeeded in making a permanent dam, tho' at the sacrifice of a good many "damns," we fear. Four times the dam broke, costing thousands of dollars to repair it, but he, and his associates, whom he had taken in as partners, heroically worked on and spent world's of cash until they finally succeeded in making a permanent dam. The river here is 400 feet wide and flows on a bed of sand nearly 30 feet deep. The dam is made of brush, rock, soil and piles, the latter driven through the immense mass of the former; on these are sleepers firmly bolted and on them are two inch pine plank firmly spiked. It is permanent.

The founder of the mill, Mr. Lanoue, has parted with his interest in it and a new company has been formed with H. M. Spalding President.

All the modern improvements for making flour have been added and it is now in every particular a first class merchant mill.

AN IMPORTANT INDUSTRY.

We have reference to the wagon manufactory and repair shop of Hull & Son on Washington, south side of the city windmill and tank.

This house has had the credit for a long time of making the best wagons in this market, and of being the best and most prompt in repairing farm machinery, and relaying and pointing plows, and with the facilities they now have they can do better work and with greater dispatch. And besides they can do a class of work, with the use of their new machinery, they could not do without it.

They have erected a fine new, iron covered fire proof building, two stories high, which gives them ample room for the conduct of their business.

They have just put in and got to running, an engine with ample power to run their machinery. Also, a large, new Screw cutting Power Lathe, of the best make. It is capable of turning a rod of iron ten feet long and cutting a screw any sized thread desired the same length. It is a very useful piece of machinery.

We may also mention their power propelled emery stones, which are of the best known make. There is also a large grindstone run by power, for grinding plows and such other articles as need grinding.

There is no class of farm machinery now except those needing castings but what this firm can repair. This will prove a great saving in time and expense to the people of this and other counties.

Too much credit cannot be given to Hull & Son for their enterprise and they should be patronized by the public. They have already expended several thousand dollars, and will make other investments and improvements as soon as a growing business shall demand.

A GOOD WORD FOR OUR ADVERTISERS.

We have not admitted to these pages all who wanted advertising space. We have exercised caution in this respect, and admitted those only whom we believe to be reliable; and so believing, we unhesitatingly recommend them to the public for their patronage.

This much for the business men.

PROFESSIONAL.

For the legal gentlemen we wish to say a good word also, and it is this:

They are the best lawyers in this city. Legal gentlemen who can be relied upon—*every time*.

Without hesitation we say of the physicians and surgeons, they have no superiors in the county. They are men who honor their profession and never shirk a duty or neglect a patient.

For all the various businesses and professions, represented in this little book, we ask the patronage of our readers, we believe them worthy of it and will deal honorably with them.

APOLOGETIC.

We set out to write this history without lionizing anyone and we feel sure that we have succeeded. But we also aimed to give due credit where credit was due and in this we feel as tho we have succeeded.

All references to the work or acts of the writer are regretfully made. It seemed however, impossible to write a truthfully history of the county without making them—we could have followed the example of others and willfully and falsely omitted such reference. The reader can skip them if he wants to without offending us.

If we appear too harsh in any remarks concerning any town or individual, we reply that the causes which provoked them were much greater and much more numerous than appear in the book.

In no case have we said any more than what seemed to us necessary to be said, and there we have stopped.

We have purposely refrained from giving credit to some parties, as "first settlers," whose over zealous friends claimed as such, and for the good and substantial reason that we *know the claim is false* of our own personal knowledge.

We set out with the intention of mentioning specially such legislative measures as the several representatives were the authors of, but could not procure the legislative records in time to do so. To all those gentlemen, however, we give the credit of doing their duty and working for, what they believed to be, the best interest of the county and State.

ERRORS.

The failure, for want of time, to read proofs the second time has been the cause of some errors, which we wish to call attention to.

On page 10, 15th line from top of first column, read "September for August.

"The correction of the officers elected (page 10) at the first election appears elsewhere.

On page 11, line 31 from bottom 2d column, for 6 read 20.

Third line below this read "John" for Henry.

Same column lines 11 and 12, read "Marling for 'Morely.'

In spelling some words we have used the phonetic system intentionally, and in some cases *unintentionally*. "Tho," "altho," "thru," "depo," "program," were purposely so spelled, but "stiring," "buffalo," "squirel," is the neglect of proof reading. We mention this for the benefit of our children readers.

The above are all the important errors that are discovered at this time and they occur in the first 16 pages which made up the first forms.

Roster of County Officers and Representatives Elected since the County was Organized.

First in order are those appointed by the Governor to or before the first election, canvass the votes cast, and declare the result.

Special Commissioners—Moses Heller, of Elk township; G. W. Wilcox, of Sibley township; Henry Lear, of Shirley township; Clerk—N. D. Hagaman, of Shirley township.*

1866.

Commissioner 1st Dist., Unknown.
    " 2d " Wm. English.
    " 3d " Robt. w. Smith.
County clerk, W. M. Wilcox.
Sheriff, Quincy Honey.
Representative, John B. Rupe,

1867

Commissioners, John McCluer, A. A. Bradfor and William English.
Clerk, Charles Davis.
Supt of schools, J. B. Rupe.
Treasurer, David Heller.
Sheriff, Quincy Honey.
Probate Judge, Ed. Neely.
Representative, J. M. Hagaman.

1868.

At this election U. S. Grant received for President 101 votes and Seymour H. J. M. Harvey, for Governor, 100 and George W. Glick 11. The rest of the state ticket ran about the same way.
Representative elect, I. N. Dalrymple.
Probate Judge, J. S. Fowler.
Commissioner 3d District, H. C. Snyder.
Surveyor, John Shearer.
County Attorney, C. M. Kellogg, of Clay Co.
County Assessor, W. H. Page.
Supt. of Schools, B. H. McEckron.

1869.

Representative, A. J. Shelhamer.
Commissioner 1st Dist., W. H. Page
    " 2d " Chester Dutton
    " 3d " John Murphy
Sheriff, George Hibner
Coroner, S M Ransopher
Clerk, E Fox
Treasurer, David Heller
Register of Deeds, J S Bowen
Surveyor, N H Billings
Probate Judge, Samuel Doran
Clerk of Dist. Court, C O Huntress
Co Attorney, Frank Cunningham, of Clay Co

1870.

Representative, B H McEckron
Clerk Dist Court, W E Reid
Probate Judge, D J Fowler
Surveyor, J O Sawin
County Supt., S. Doran
[County Attorney, L Westover

1871.

Representative, B H McEckron
Sheriff, J M Woodward
Coroner, D B Dutton
Commissioner st Dist., David Turner
    " 2d " Wm English,
    " 3d " H C Synder
Treasurer, W J Campbell
Register of Deeds, J S Bowen

*As the townships now are; there were no townships then in the county.
Election ordered for the first Tuesday after the first Monday in November, the general election day.

County Clerk, W E Reid
Surveyor, Samuel Doran

1872

Representative, H C Snyder
Probate Judge, C W McDonald
Clerk Dist. Court, W E Reid
County Attorney, H A Hunter
County Supt, S Doran
Coroner, D C Atwater
Commissioner 3rd Dist., G W Carver

1873.

Representative, B H McEckron
Sheriff, J M Woodward
Coroner, Wm McK Burns
Commissioner 1st Dist., Frank Gagnon
    " 2d " W M Wilcox
    " 3d " Elam Pease
Treasurer, W J Campbell,
Register of Deeds. Milton Reasoner
Surveyor, L H Smyth
County Clerk, W E Reid

1874.

Representative 82d Dist., C K Wells
    " 81-t "
Probate Judge, J L Sturges
Clerk Dist Court, C F Hostetler
County Supt, Samuel Doran
County Attorney, H A Hunter

1875.

Representative, Geo N Nichols
County Attorney, F W Sturges
Sheriff, John D Wilson
Coroner, Nathaniel Fox
Commissioner 1st Dist., W S Cramp
    " 2d " E E Swearngin
    " 3d " Enos Rushton
Clerk, Edmund Martin
Treasurer, W E Reid
Register of Deeds. Milton Reasoner
Surveyor, L H Smyth
Attorney, Theodore Laing
Probate Judge, F W Sturges, appointed to fill vacancy

1876.

Representative 102d Dist., D C McKay
    " 13d " C W McDonald
Probate Judge, S D Houston, Jr
Clerk of Court, C F Hostetler
Superintendent, J C Dana
County Attorney, F W Sturges

1877.

Sheriff, John D Wilson
County Clerk, E E Swearngin
Register of Deeds, C W Whipp
Commissioner 1st Dist., J M Gillespie
    " 2d " C N Moore
    " 3d " A H Spaulding
Coroner, J G Gilmer
Surveyor, L H Smyth
Treasurer, W E Reid

1878.

Clerk Dist. court, C F Hostetler
County Attorney, Theo Laing
Superintendent, W T Root
Probate Judge, S D Houston. Jr
Commissioner 1st Dist, Charles Proctor
Representative 10 d Dist, D C McKay
    " 103 " Joseph Cool

1879.

Treasurer, H M Spalding
Clerk, E E Swearngin
Register of Deeds, C W Whipp
Sheriff, D C Wilson
Surveyor, R S McCrary
Coroner, H E Smith
Commissioner 2 D Dist, C F Moore

1880.

Clerk of Court, C F Hostetler
Probate Judge, W F Compton
County Attorney, Theo Laing
Superintendent, W T Root
Coroner, S H Pratt
Commissioner 3d Dist. J F Hannum
Representative 102d Dist. W S Cramp .

" 1063 " Joseph Cool

1-81.

Treasurer, E E Swearngin
County Clerk, N H ustine
Sheriff, John D Wilson
Register of Deeds, C W Whipp
Surveyor, Jacob Short
Coroner, S H Pratt
Commissioner 1st Dist, L B Wilcox

1882.

Representative 81st Dist, L W Borton
" 82 " F W Sturges
County Attorney, J W Sheafor
Probate Judge, D L Brown
Superintendent, W C Cook
Clerk of Court, C F Hostetler
Commissioner 2d List, J C Gafford

1883.

Treasurer, E E Swearngin
Clerk, L N Horton
Register of Deeds, A H Spaulding
Sheriff, John D Wilson
Coroner, D W Lee
Surveyor, Samuel Moran
Commission r 1st Dist, A M Lafond
" 2d " Carr Brown

1884.

Representative 81st Dist, G M Kreger
" 8 d " H B Moore
Clerk of Court, C F Hostetler
County Attorney, J W Sheafor
Probate Judge, D L Brown
Superintendent, T W Roach
Commissioner 1st Dist, A M Lafond
" 2d " Benjamin Lake

ORGANIZATION OF CITIES.

CONCORDIA, 3d class, August 7th 1872
CLYDE,   "   "   1874
JAMESTOWN,   "   July 6th 1883
MILTONVALE,   "   October 6th 1883

PRESIDENTIAL VOTE—1864–1884.

1864

LINCOLN, A., Rep................. 25
McCLELLAN, GEO. B. Dem.,........ 2
     Maj.................... 23

1868

GRANT, U. S., Rep................. 100
SEYMOUR, HORATIO, Dem.......... 11
     Maj...................., ... 89

1872

GRANT, U. S. Rep................. 920
GREELEY, HORACE, Liberal Rep.... 260
     Maj.................... 660

1876

HAYES, R. B. Rep................. 1,184
TILDEN, S. J. Dem................ 489
     Maj.................... 695
COOPER, PETER, Greenback........ 7

1880

GARFIELD, J. A. Rep............. 2,156
HANCOCK, W. S. Dem............. 888
     Maj.................... 1,268
WEAVER, J. B. Greenback........ 65

1884

BLAINE, J. G. Rep............,,,,...... 2,692
CLEVELAND, GROVER Dem......... 1,155
     Maj.................... 1,537
ST. JOHN, J. P. Prohibition....... 223
BUTLER, B. F. Greenback......... 91
     Maj.................... 132
     BLAINE over all............... 1,213

CLOUD COUNTY.

AREA.—LANDS CULTIVATED AND NOT
CULTIVATED. — AGRICULTURAL PRO-
DUCTS.—CORN, CATTLE, HOGS, SHEEP,
&C., &C.

No. of square miles in county,   720
" " acres in the county,   460,800
" " " cultivation 1884,   190,083
" " " uncultivated 1884,   270,717
" " " of corn 1884,   131,576
" " " wheat, "   13,411
" " " rye, "   7,005
" " " oats, "   16,915
" " " potatoes, "   1,633
" " " broom corn,   2,359
" ;" " Sugar cane,   401
" " " all other produce,   181
" " heads of horses,   8,435
" " " mules,   714
" " " cattle,   22,453
" " " hogs,   47,703
" " " sheep,   17,812
" " school houses,   103
" " churches,   12
" " Organized cities in 1884,   5
" " miles wagon road in Co.,   15,00
" " " Republican river in Co.,   75
" " " Solomon river in Co.,   20
" miles railroad in county, Central
   Branch,   32
Union Pacific,   16
Republican valley branch C. B.,   6
Jewell branch C. B.,   6
Solomon branch U. P.,   16
Lawrenceburg branch U. P.,   3
Burlington & Missouri,   8
Kansas Central,   5

ANNUAL ASSESSMENT FOR 24 YEARS.

1860*..........	1872.......$740,306.08
1861*..........	1873.......751,580.00
1862†......$3,000	1874.......904,545.00
1863†..... 5,000	1875.......754,637.00
1864†..... 8,000	1876.......783,848.00
1865†.....11,000	1877.......909,026.00
1866†.....18,000	1878.......1,212,830.07
1867.....31,198	1879.......1,633,162
1868...40,066.25	1880.......2,016,799
1869...80,418.60	1881.......2,145,675
1870...165,908.25	1882.......2,376,672
1871...422,551.00	1883.......2,591,765
	1884....$2,938,771.

* No assessment.
† Give from memory. Was assessed by
Washington county, but the records were burnt
when the Treasurer's office of that county was
burned.
‡ Estimated assessment.

Township Officers, 1884.

Township.	Trustee.	Clerk.	Treasurer.	Justices.	Pop.
Ar n	W M Wilcox	Wm McNelly	G W Dodk	H J Wright F S Wallace	693
Aurora.....	F A Thomps'n	E Letourneau	Jos Dugas	F A Thompson H H Frazier	652
Buffalo.....	Jno Millirons	John McCowen	Jesse Woods	J H McCoy U Saepherd	790
Center.....	John Myers	D W Ball	J C Carter	Thos Livengood W F Compton	881
Colfax......	A Morriset	W C Campbell	I T Williams	J W McDonald W C Campbell	717
Elk	E R DeBray	T W Roach	P McDonald	R A McCord I N Page	2235
Grant......	N M French	L S Kroetch	R M Staley	D W Peterson P A Thomas	1213
Lawrence..	W Bramwell	Jacob Short	Walter Lawry	Jacob Short J W Campbell	655
Lincoln	W H Wright	John Linton	C F Hostetler	A B Chaffee Anderson	3222
Lyon	A W Bickford	H P Blake	Thos Bue	P E Butler A C Predmore	876
Meredith...	John Carver	H H Yount	S S C	J W Elliott Abner Coffin	568
Nelson.....	David Pinney	J B Campbell	H B ervin	H H Young W A Pierce	696
Oakland ...	Montgomery	F J Gildersleve	Wm Ferguson	Geo M Kreger Job Gildersleve	524
Shirley.....	J M Ijames	Eli Laceyer	S Sevey	J S Perry	1052
Sibley......	C V Miller	S J Roberts	G G Murdock	S P Linn L B Hay	642
Solomon...	Jacob Studt	A Ott	C A Godley	Wm Butler Ed Jones	1173
Summit....	M D Sutherlin	S D Potter	A S Wilson	A Montgomery Wm Rhodes	881
Starr.......	James Neill	B H Howe	O A Loomis	A B Fry J W Shay	978

Total population of the county 1884, - - 18,448

NEWSPAPERS.

THE KANSAS BLADE. J. M. & J. E. Hagaman, editors, publishers and proprietors.

The *Concordia Empire.* Empire Printing Company, C. W. McDonald, editor.

The *Concordia Times.* Chas. J. English, editor and proprietor.

The *Cloud County Critic.* Thomas Owen, jr., editor, Concordia.

The *Clyde Herald.* Jona B. Rupe, editor and proprietor, Clyde.

The *Clyde Mail.* J. C. Cline & Sons, editors and proprietors Clyde.

The *Glasco Sun.* Ferd Prince, editor and proprietor, Glasco.

The *Miltonvale News.* Pinkerton & McDonald, editors and proprietors, Miltonvale.

The *Jamestown Kansan.* James and Mary Burton, editors, Jamestown.

CHURCHES OF CLOUD COUNTY.

Baptist: Organizations, 3; membership 109; church edifices, 2; value of church property, $4,000. Church of Christ: Organizations, 5; membership, 350; church edifices, 2; value of church property, $2,500. Lutheran: Organizations, 1; membership, 160. Methodist Episcopal: Organizations, 13; membership, 460; church edifices, 5; value of church property, $10,000. Presbyterian: Organizations, 7; membership, 252; church edifices, 4; value of church property, $12,500. Roman Catholic: Organizations, 5; membership, 1,600; church edifices, 2; value of church property, $5,000. United Presbyterian: Organizations, 1; membership, 53. Congregational: Organizations, 1; membership, 8.

Map of Cloud County, Kansas.

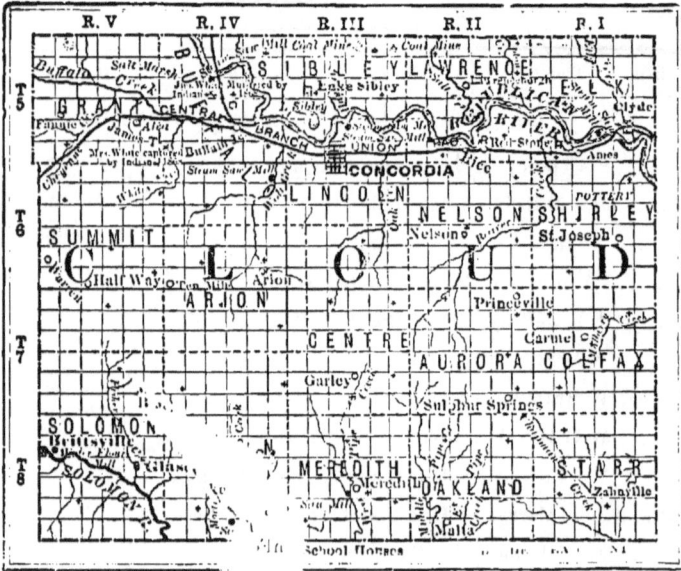

CONGRESSIONAL TOWNSHIP MAP.

Township............ ....Range...........
....County,..........

16th and 36th sections of each Congressional Township are set aside for school purposes.

www.ingramcontent.com/pod-product-compliance
Lightning Source LLC
Chambersburg PA
CBHW022150090426
42742CB00010B/1456